Perfect
Empowerment

Perfect Empowerment

ALL YOU NEED
TO GET IT RIGHT
FIRST TIME

SARAH COOK AND
STEVE MACAULAY

ARROW

Published by Arrow Books in 1996

1 3 5 9 10 8 6 4 2

First published by
Arrow Books Limited
20 Vauxhall Bridge Road, London SW1V 2SA

Random House Australia (Pty) Limited
16 Dalmore Drive, Scoresby
Victoria 3179, Australia

Random House New Zealand Limited
18 Poland Road, Glenfield
Auckland 10, New Zealand

Random House South Africa (Pty) Limited
Box 2263, Rosebank 2121, South Africa

Papers used by Random House UK Limited are natural, recyclable
products made from wood grown in sustainable forests. The
manufacturing processes conform to the environmental regulations
of the country of origin.

Companies, institutions and other organizations wishing to make bulk
purchases of any business books published by Random House should
contact their local bookstore or Random House direct:
Special Sales Director
Random House
20 Vauxhall Bridge Road
London SW1V 2SA
Tel: 0171 973 9670 Fax: 0171 828 6681

Random House UK Limited Reg. No. 954009
ISBN 0 09 966981 1

Set in Bembo by SX Composing DTP, Rayleigh, Essex
Printed and bound in Great Britain by
Cox & Wyman Ltd, Reading, Berkshire

ABOUT THE AUTHORS

Sarah Cook is Director of The Stairway Consultancy. Her company specializes in helping organizations increase their level of empowerment and customer service.

Current projects include work in retail, financial, pharmaceutical, health and manufacturing sectors.

Sarah is the author of a number of publications on customer service and empowerment. *Perfect Empowerment* is her fifth book.

Steve Macaulay has over 20 years' experience working with organizations to achieve empowered cultures. This experience spans a wide range of sectors and organizations.

Steve is currently engaged on a major change project with an airline which involves a substantial shift in the level of empowerment.

Sarah and Steve can be contacted at:
The Stairway Consultancy
35 Montpelier Vale
London SE3 0TJ
Tel: 0181 297 0333

ACKNOWLEDGEMENTS

The authors express their grateful thanks to the many businesses who have allowed their journeys towards empowerment to provide examples for this book.

They also thank the following for giving permission:

Arrow Books Limited for the quotation from *Maverick* by Ricardo Semler, 1993.

Currency Doubleday for the quotation from *Control Your Destiny or Someone Else Will* by J. Welch, N.M. Tichy and S. Sherman, 1993.

Ebury Press for the quotation from *Body and Soul* by Anita Roddick, 1991.

The Financial Times for the quotation from article by Tony Jackson and Andrew Gowers, 21 December 1995

Harvard Business Press for the quotation from *The Wisdom of Teams* by J. Katzenbach and D. Smith

Kogan Page for the quotation from *Practical Business Re-engineering* by Nick Oblensky, 1994.

CONTENTS

INTRODUCTION

Empowerment has become one of the dominant management themes of the 90s. Is it just another example of empty management rhetoric? We suggest in this book that empowerment provides a practical philosophy and a tool for change which helps improve both customer and employee satisfaction, and therefore the effectiveness of the organization. Plenty of managers have misused the term, but this should not obscure the benefits of true empowerment.

People on the outside have little difficulty in recognising an empowered organization. They do so through the way it does business. It all seems straightforward . . . but if you set out to empower your organization, the process can be anything but easy.

The aim of the book is to help you to weigh up the benefits of empowerment and make a realistic assessment of some of the difficulties of putting it into practice. We also examine why empowerment is not appropriate for all organizations.

The book contains the results of the experiences of organizations which have taken the empowerment path, with varying degrees of success. In some of these cases, the success achieved has brought about transformation – more prosperity, greater vitality, growth – as well as sought for change in levels of quality. In others, it has meant the ability to continue in an ever more competitive world.

Few of these companies have found the process painless, because everyone involved has to adjust to a new way of doing business – of taking decisions and working more independently. Their experience, however painful, can help you. You may also be encouraged to learn of the more exciting, positive experiences which have unlocked the potential previously suppressed by traditional constraining management controls. This has positively affected the bottom line.

Perfect Empowerment is targeted generally towards people who are about to embark on the empowerment process, who are weighing up whether to do so or not, or who are curious to learn more about the substance behind the buzzword.

If you are a senior manager in an organization, this may be you. You are faced with the need to take a fresh look at change, perhaps because you want to make more of opportunities available to you, or are running out of ideas for improving cost effectiveness through conventional means, or because your margins are getting tighter, or you feel the competition nibbling at your heels. *Should empowerment form part of your strategy for the future?*

If you are a middle manager in an organization, you may feel that your people offer more potential to meet opportunities than is being achieved. The days of generous budgets are gone, but the demands for improved results keep coming. Customer and quality expectations are ever-rising; people want more quality, personal service which meets their needs more closely. *You may be thinking that empowerment could be a means of 'doing more with less'.*

If you are a front line team leader, your employees are probably no longer prepared to be 'yes-men'. They are more likely to challenge authority – yours or top management's – and with the rising pace of change, you feel that you can no longer be the expert on everything. Is there any way of tapping the energy you see around you? You are getting pressure to work to lean budgets while being ever-more productive. *Could empowerment help in this situation?*

Reading this book will help to suggest why empowerment has captured the imagination of many organizations who seek to achieve perhaps the most important goal of all: *meeting customer needs effectively and profitably in a fast-changing world.*

WHY EMPOWERMENT

Empowerment is a significant means of improving business performance through devolving decision making and responsibility, thus encouraging employee involvement. Numerous organizations have found that it brings closeness to the customer. A major benefit is the increased energy it generates and the greater commitment of employees through their ownership of decisions affecting the workplace.

WHAT IS EMPOWERMENT?

A woman went into a food store to buy some ingredients for a special meal she was preparing that evening. On returning home she discovered that the cream she had just purchased was sour, although the sell-by date on the packaging indicated it should still be fresh.

She phoned the store and explained her predicament. It was too late for her to go back to the store and still prepare her meal. She complained that the store should ensure in future that the cream was fresh and, leaving her name and address, she was offered a refund and a sincere apology.

Imagine the customer's surprise when, twenty minutes after phoning, she opened the door to the member of staff who had answered her telephone call. He had decided to make an apology in person on behalf of the store, and to bring her two replacement cartons of fresh cream so that her dinner party could go ahead.

This epitomizes empowered behaviour: an employee has the authority and takes the initiative to do what is necessary, going beyond the call of duty.

Jan Carlzon, former CEO of SAS Scandinavian Airlines

describes empowerment as: 'To free someone from rigorous control . . . and to give that person freedom to take responsibility for his ideas, decisions, actions.'

Empowerment is a change of management philosophy which helps create an environment where every individual can use his or her abilities and energies to meet organizational goals. It is a method of encouraging initiative and responsiveness, so that matters are addressed and resolved as quickly and flexibly as possible at the point where the issue is spotted. Staff are free to take decisions without referring upwards or fearing repercussions from their manager.

HOW IS THE EMPOWERED ORGANIZATION MORE EFFECTIVE?

In an empowered organization, individuals are respected for the important part they play in its success. They have the authority and flexibility to ensure they deliver results to a high standard and no-one is constantly checking to make sure this is so. An empowered organization is often easy to do business with: its entire manner of working is geared towards taking responsibility. Where there are difficulties, they are sorted out quickly.

In an empowered company people don't hide. They share responsibility for problems and are proactive in working together to resolve issues. People outside the organization have little trouble recognizing empowerment through the way they are treated. Individual employees' attitudes towards them are personal and positive.

The Marriott chain of hotels makes a proud statement of its employees' empowerment through its advertizements. A customer who can't sleep is found the right brand of drinking chocolate by an employee who goes halfway across town to get it. A lost wallet is returned after endless trouble on the initiative of a porter. The desk clerk lends a Washington guest his new trainers so that the guest can go for a run with the President.

W H Smith has empowered staff to decide whether to exchange a product or refund a customer's money without reference to a manager. W H Smith sees the return as staff putting more energy and effectiveness into the business.

The US store Nordstrom adopts a simple, over-riding philosophy instead of detailed rules:

1.   Use your good judgement at all times
2.   There are no additional rules

This approach to setting rules benefits the company because staff do more than merely what is needed and deliver something special, overcoming bottlenecks and taking extra trouble.

The Brazilian manufacturing company Semco transformed itself from a highly traditional small company into a much larger, fast-growing profitable enterprise. It achieved this through bold empowerment: employees are given the authority to set production quotas, help redesign products, influence marketing and even determine their own pay levels. Chief Executive Ricardo Semler built up the company by being a catalyst for others to make decisions. For him, *'Success means not making decisions myself.'*

Harvester Restaurants recast a moderately successful operation into a more profitable, growing business by reducing the layers of management and trusting day-to-day management issues to self-managing teams.

What does empowerment mean to the employee?
Within an organizational context, empowerment may mean different things to different people. Some definitions of empowerment from a cross-section of employees in one organization included:

'Devolving responsibility to front line staff'
'Being accountable for decisions'
'Empowerment is a state of mind – it allows you to be an individual'
'It's about flattening the organization'
'Empowerment is another term for delegation'
'Knowing what your customer wants and expects and going all out to achieve this'
'Taking decisions away from managers and letting people direct their own work flow'
'It's an excuse to reduce staff'

The word 'empowerment' is trumpeted from the board-rooms of many organizations. Yet it is often used as a justification to keep everything intact but to cut back staff and layers of management, reduce costs and take selective action in a piecemeal way. Employees quickly see the reality. One employee in a major multi-national commented: 'In this brave new world we are "empowered" to do things, then someone says "are you sure you've got the costs right?" '

A new approach to managing
A commonly held misconception is that empowerment is just a 'fad' word for delegation. In fact, there are many differences between delegation and empowerment. At the root of these differences is a shift in approach to managing.

Managers who delegate a task give employees the responsibility and authority to complete the task, but accountability for the task remains their own.

In an empowered organization the manager relinquishes responsibility, authority *and* accountability. Managers become coaches and facilitators, not controllers who keep people on short leashes. The following gives an indication of the contrast between the two approaches of management style, empowerment and command and control:

Individual decides what needs to be done within agreed parameters	v.	Manager decides what needs to be done
Individual has accountability	v.	Manager retains accountability
Manager acts as coach	v.	Manager supervises output
Information flows freely	v.	Information is restricted
Individual is proactive	v.	Individual is reactive
Likely to be more outward looking and flexible	v.	Inward looking and rigid

On the other hand, empowerment is not about letting people go their own way without responsibility or agreed standards. It is operating independently but against agreed values or guidelines. Staff at Harvester Restaurants, for example, are given a lot of personal discretion, but not to redesign the menu, set prices or change the decor. A common brand identity is seen as too important.

Empowerment is not appropriate to all organizations. Those who need absolute uniformity would find empowerment more difficult to introduce. Those who must exercise very tight regulatory control need to set careful boundaries. For example, in 1995 Barings Bank collapsed because of what was widely felt to be lax supervision by the management of one of its traders, Nick Leeson, who lost a massive £900 million and brought the bank to financial ruin.

Genuine empowerment takes time but it will ripple through the organization and lead to change in every part of it. For example, Frizzell Financial Services experienced some difficulties when it first introduced the concept of empowerment. Productivity dropped initially but enthusiasts outweighed detractors and after a period the company began to benefit. There must have been some anxious eyes

on the bottom line whilst this was taking place. Some organizations may not be prepared to face the disruption which
empowerment brings.

How much involvement in decision making can employees have?

The degree of empowerment within an organization will
usually represent a choice across a spectrum. Organizations
often choose to move progressively along the spectrum as
they become more empowered.

1. **At one end, decisions are made by managers,
    but suggestions are invited from employees.** For
    example, it is said that McDonald's have usefully
    gleaned ideas from staff that have been translated into
    such popular products as the Big Mac, the McBLT and
    the Egg McMuffin. Members of staff at Marks &
    Spencers came up with the idea of enhancing the sales
    of its speciality foods by linking products from the
    same country as part of its in-store promotions.

2. **In the middle of the spectrum, day-to-day oper-
    ations are organized by employee groups, for
    example shift rotas, but managers still take more
    fundamental strategic decisions.** Key decision
    making rests with managers, who determine strategy,
    budgets, and future plans. Marriott Hotels, for
    example, have devolved many of the day-to-day deci-
    sions to their staff whilst managers retain a strategic
    overview.

    At Novotel general managers are given autonomy on
    how to run their hotel but they still work within a
    basic corporate framework to maintain the essential
    principles and identity of Novotel.

3. **At the other end of the continuum, self-directed
    teams network together.** All decision making, short

and long term, is devolved to team level.

Empowerment is most visible throughout the organization in stages two and three. Only a few organizations have gone as far as three in the UK. In the US there are more examples, such as jeans manufacturer Levi Strauss who has devolved many important decisions to its self-managing teams.

National & Provincial Building Society created self-managing teams at all levels of the organization to help create a customer focus. Other companies such as Xerox and Sun Live have developed self-managing teams in various parts of their organizations. These teams are often found in discrete areas of the business and work alongside traditional structures.

The starting point for beginning the process of empowerment should be an honest assessment of the current culture within your organization. This assessment will lead to a wider awareness of what needs to change and why, and the potential barriers. Empowerment will not occur just because senior managers tell their employees they are now 'empowered' and then work things out as they go along. It is a process which needs a thorough plan, with thought given to mechanisms for constant monitoring and reinforcement. Planning will not guarantee success but it does provide a basis to set milestones and measure achievements.

THE STARTING POINT – ASSESSING YOUR CURRENT LEVEL OF EMPOWERMENT

The impetus for beginning the process of empowerment may come from outside the company, for example increased pressure to provide outstanding customer service, or within the organization, for example changes in senior management, cost cutting or restructuring. Whatever the catalyst, the first step is to assess where your organization is in terms of its culture and the way things are done within the company. Once this has been achieved, you will have a better picture of what needs to change and the degree of change you desire as an organization.

Kent County Council recognized the need to take action to change from a traditional, centralized structure into a more empowered one which they defined as devolved, customer orientated and flexible. They identified communications, involvement and a 'customer first' attitude as the keys to change. Annual MORI surveys of customers' perceptions have been initiated to demonstrate improvements in service quality and the way the organization has changed towards a more empowered culture.

Conducting an audit

In assessing an organization's current level of empowerment, it is common for a company to conduct a survey of
its employees to diagnose how involved they feel in the
way the organization is run.

Multinational Ciba-Geigy allows its business units great
independence. In 1990 a 'Vision 2000' was developed for
the future of the company and the organization was restruc-
tured into 14 business units. Empowerment was central to
the vision, but each business unit was given the autonomy
to begin this process as and when it wished. To help establish the degree of empowerment which employees believe
they have and the changes in their perceptions, Ciba UK
conducts an annual attitude survey. The survey asks individuals to rate the behaviour of their manager in helping
them become empowered against eight 'dimensions':

My Manager:
- Ensures openness
- Delegates authority
- Manages performance
- Develops people
- Promotes co-operation
- Communicates efficiently
- Encourages innovation
- Resolves issues

The managers rate themselves against these dimensions too.
Managers' scores are then compared with their subordinates' perceptions and each manager analyses the gap so that
they know what he or she has to do to help create a more
empowered climate. The organization believes the survey
is a useful way of setting action plans. The survey is conducted at all levels of the organization, so that all opinions
are canvassed.

Here is an example of a short audit which can be given to

employees as part of the assessment process. We suggest you use this model as a starting point for discussion. You can build on the questions and add more in the areas you and your team feel are critical indicators. It focuses on employees' perceptions.

Example of Cultural Audit	**Degree of Agreement**			
Circle the degree of your agreement in response to each statement	*Agree strongly*	*Agree*	*Disagree*	*Disagree strongly*
1. I understand the goals and objectives of the organization.	1	2	3	4
2. I have a good understanding of the ways in which I contribute to the success of the organization.	1	2	3	4
3. I understand my own role and responsibilities.	1	2	3	4
4. The objectives of my work team are clear.	1	2	3	4
5. My work colleagues co-operate with me.	1	2	3	4
6. My manager listens to my ideas.	1	2	3	4
7. I have the support and trust of my manager to help me perform my job well.	1	2	3	4
8. I have sufficient information to allow me to perform my job efficiently.	1	2	3	4
9. I am encouraged to take responsibility for my job.	1	2	3	4
10. I receive regular feedback on my performance.	1	2	3	4

11. I have sufficient training to help me perform my job well.	1	2	3	4
12. I am encouraged to develop personally at work.	1	2	3	4
13. My manager supports my decisions.	1	2	3	4
14. I can influence decisions which affect my work.	1	2	3	4
15. I understand the needs of my customers.	1	2	3	4
16. I am rewarded fairly for my efforts.	1	2	3	4
17. I feel proud to work for the organization.	1	2	3	4
18. Innovation is encouraged in my job.	1	2	3	4
19. The organization has changed positively in the past twelve months.	1	2	3	4
20. I feel that I can express my honest opinion to my manager.	1	2	3	4
Total score				

Score 40 or under: Your organization fosters the right climate to encourage empowerment. Make a note of the strong areas in the survey and the areas where you may wish to act to reduce barriers to empowerment.

Score 41 or over: This result indicates that much more can be done within your organization to empower employees. Study the scores and pick out themes which will help you draw up your priorities for action.

The Automobile Association is one of the many organizations which conduct annual employee surveys to assess the cultural factors which help or hinder empowerment, thus gaining a measure of how well it is achieving the goal of empowerment. Surveys soon lose 'bite' if they are not followed up, *so they must become part of an action plan which is pursued vigorously.*

The UK arm of computer software company Microsoft was disappointed to find that the first attempts to empower its employees were unsuccessful. As regular surveys picked up, employees felt that they had been given greater responsibility but not the authority to carry out this wider role. Also, some saw empowerment as a passing management fad, so it was not worth investing much time and energy in it. The surveys provided Microsoft with evidence of the need to redefine the areas in which it could realistically give its employees both authority and responsibility. This mechanism spurred managers into taking a fresh look at how they could make empowerment work.

Mining and construction equipment manufacturer Caterpillar set up structured brainstorming sessions at one of its US plants to pick out ways of overcoming the main blockages to empowerment. The output of the brainstorming was refined to isolate ten elements of an empowered environment.

One of the main purposes of such information gathering is to identify likely barriers and blockages to introducing empowerment and the implications of changes. A survey will often conclude that different groups have varying responses to empowerment. Senior managers usually respond more positively than other groups in such surveys. Middle managers are often the least responsive to empowerment. Individual contributors may be cautious about deciding more things on their own authority (as was demonstrated at Microsoft), without some clear indications that this initiative is not just 'another project'.

It is unrealistic to expect everyone to welcome empowerment unreservedly or to change their behaviour even if
they do. In planning for empowerment, organizations
should plan for differences in the pace of change. *Help and
support will be needed to coach people through the process and to
build confidence and trust.*

In the US, extensive research at glass manufacturer Viking
Glass identified mistrust between employees and managers
as the number one barrier to empowerment. The route to
change developed by the company was based on a strategy
containing three elements to overcome this block: sticking
to promises, treating people as equal, and consistency and
thoroughness in its management practices. Evidence of
ways to demonstrate this in practice was thought through
beforehand. This ensured that managers lived up to the
promise of openness and involved people as equals, giving
the same commitment and persistent messages to all
employees, not just certain groups.

IDENTIFYING WHAT NEEDS TO CHANGE

After the initial diagnosis, the next task is to confirm how
far your organization wants to go along the spectrum of
empowerment, and therefore what needs to change in the
way employees go about their work.

A financial services company undertook a diagnostic review
by holding discussions and completing a cultural survey
amongst all its staff. Here are some of the findings which
came out of the analysis:

Factors which help empowerment
- New management team beginning to canvass staff
  opinion
- Leadership programme emphasises need to take
  responsibility

- One function already acts as a self-managing team
- Competitors react speedily to customer requests and we recognize we need to match their speed

Factors which hinder empowerment
- Historically, lack of involvement of middle managers who are important in decision-making
- 'Them and us' attitude between certain groups of employees
- Costs saving seen to be more important than individual's personal needs
- 'Blame' culture

As a result of this analysis, the company identified a number of factors which it needed to change in its working practices to encourage greater employee involvement and initiative. Here is an example of some of the factors which it decided needed addressing:

- Clearer understanding of organizational mission and values
- More focus on customer needs – both internal and external
- Greater emphasis on training and development
- Increased inter-department communication

The next step was a more detailed action plan around each area with a strong commitment from everyone to make the change happen.

CREATING A FRAMEWORK FOR ACTION
In this section we set out some frameworks or guidelines for action which we have found useful to reduce what can be a daunting task to something manageable.

For empowerment to be successful, it must become part of *how* everyone goes about their job. This means that a fundamental value of the organization must be the recognition that **the development of the performance of a company is linked directly to unlocking the performance of its people.**

Car rental company Avis has published a framework for its empowerment process which is founded on the belief that employees need clearly defined authority and the skills to take decisions confidently. The culture is one where employees will be trusted to take the right decisions and as a result employees will take responsibility for their actions and seek out opportunities to put empowerment into practice. This framework is based on the acronym ACTORS:

- **A**uthority
- **C**onfidence and competence
- **T**rust
- **O**pportunities
- **R**esponsibility
- **S**upport

Eight key steps
In the authors' experience of helping a wide range of organizations to increase the scope and levels of empowerment, there are eight key steps to take in working towards successful empowerment.

1. Link to a vision
Link empowerment to the organization's vision and values. Unless empowerment is seen as underpinning the organization's vision, employees may view it as a 'management fad' or miss the context of its introduction. Empowerment must become part of the organization's values so that it is perceived to be linked intrinsically to organizational success. Harvester Restaurants has tied its empowerment process very firmly to its mission and values. All employees attend a one day training seminar where they explore what the mission and values mean to them.

2. Lead by example

The manner of leading the process is critical: empowerment must be seen to come from the top. Whilst this may seem to contradict what empowerment is about, leaders can provide a vision for the future and give the support and encouragement which are so vital to creating the environment where people take charge of their own destiny. In addition, the empowerment process should encourage champions who can in turn lead the process throughout all parts of the organization. Bill Hewlett, founder of Hewlett-Packard has set the tone for his organization by proclaiming in words and deeds the importance of the individual, who will do a good and creative job if given the right environment.

3. Communicate in abundance

Communication and involvement are key. Jack Welch at GE in the US says *'Communication is an attitude, an environment'*. The better the quality of information an individual receives, the better he or she can perform in the job. Through involving employees in regular communication and feedback sessions organizations can encourage empowerment. Welch describes communication as a *'constant interactive process aimed at consensus'*.

4. Review organizational structure

Organizational structures can be strait-jackets or enablers. Successful empowerment calls for changes to take place in the structure so that individuals become closer to the point of decisions, and bureaucracy can be discarded through smaller chains of control. Tom Peters says 55 per cent of an organization's success is down to its structure. However, don't fall into the common trap of *assuming* that all you need to do is create a new organization and empowerment will somehow happen.

5. Strengthen teamwork

Empowerment requires support. Empowering teamwork is

one of the strongest mechanisms for providing an environment to take initiatives and occasionally make mistakes, but to also learn from these. Empowerment can happen without teamwork, although teams often provide a supportive environment for the individual and generate more powerful results. Stamco, a small timber merchants, have encouraged teams to decide their own informal disciplinary actions and working hours as a natural extension of a *culture of ownership of issues,* and for employees to ask for what they want without close supervision.

6. Encourage personal development

People need help and encouragement to build their confidence in making their own decisions. This means not only providing training and coaching people to take on wider roles, but also demonstrating trust and respect for the individual. At a British Energy power station the annual maintenance shutdown is now run by a cross-functional team from all levels. Such a change needed management commitment, training and fact-finding visits. It has paid off handsomely. The time out of service has been nearly halved, lost generation capacity cut and huge sums saved.

7. Make customer service a focus

An end result of empowerment is very often an increased level of service to the customer. Therefore, employees at the front line and all those with internal customers should be encouraged to take responsibility for satisfying the customer.

8. Measure progress and recognise and reward success

Before beginning the process of empowerment, an organization needs to establish measures of success and to help these measures to be understood and agreed with each person. It needs to establish how it will recognise success in individuals and teams in terms of money and in other ways.

The Benefits Agency has been successful in adopting empowerment as a route to providing a more flexible and less bureaucratic service which responds to client needs. In preparing for the process, teams within the organization created an empowerment checklist and published this widely. This took the form of an 'Empowerment Chart' which outlined graphically the behaviour which employees believed would lead to empowerment.

Behaviour	leads to	Feeling of empowerment	leads to	Positive actions
	leads to		leads to	
My manager is accessible and approachable	leads to	I feel good about coming to work	leads to	I tell my boss more readily when staff and customers are not responding well to an initiative
Mistakes are used to learn, not to punish	leads to	I see my manager as a resource I use when I need to	leads to	I sort things out with colleagues without involving my manager

Setting a timetable

The development of empowerment plans helps the organization set definite milestones and targets, both short-term and longer-term, of what it wants to achieve. It means that there is a time frame for achieving these.

How long should empowerment take?

Realistically, cultural change, which is implicit within the empowerment process, takes a number of years. Experts talk of anything from two to five years to achieve fundamental change. It is useful, therefore, to set achievable short and medium-term targets as motivators and measures of progress. For example:

First three months

Conduct attitude survey and focus groups. Run workshops with all managers to create awareness of empowerment.

Second three months

Train/coach front-line staff. Initiate cross-functional project groups. Set up pilot performance management programme.

Third three months

Establish self-managing teams in some parts of the business.

3

LEADING THE PROCESS

In an empowered culture there is no place for the kind of old-style manager who is bureaucratic, inflexibly 'by the book', hierarchical, risk averse and more likely to blame than praise.

Rover Group sums up the key principles and qualities of its empowering leaders (those who empower others) as:

- Business leaders, people who understand the whole business
- People oriented
- Promote teamworking
- Encourage broad roles, with themselves as role models
- Recognise success not status

The experience of empowered organizations suggests **leadership is a key factor in generating enthusiasm and commitment.** Top leaders can do much to transform organizations, but in the end leadership has to be present throughout the organization.

EMPOWERING LEADER VS. TRADITIONAL MANAGER

In a traditional organizational environment, leadership comes from senior managers who set up a chain of command reaching from the top to the most junior of the management team. Seven levels of management is not at all uncommon. Management in this hierarchical structure can be characterised by:

- Micro management of every detail
- Power and decision making concentrated in the hands of the manager
- Controls based on lack of trust – little discretion given

- Information flowing largely one way
- An aura of infallibility surrounding the manager
- Goals set *for* individuals not *by* the people who have to achieve them
- Performance management is a one-way process of controlling, checking and reviewing

Rover Group has portrayed this approach as a traditional pyramid where the top five per cent have all the ideas – managers and supervisors set all the standards which in turn become ceilings which disempower every employee. But as a leading management consultant comments *'Old fashioned management is easier than the new leadership'*, where there are less simple relationships.

In an empowered environment there are many leaders at all levels of the organization working towards a common aim. There are also typically far fewer levels of management. Members of the workforce are the experts feeding ideas to management. Managers then become enablers, helping to free up resources and acting for the teams as facilitators. This means that:

- Authority is devolved to the point closest to the work
- Managers become coaches, helping others to succeed
- Managers act as champions of their teams
- Information is encouraged to flow freely within a team and outside it
- The manager helps his or her team to be part of the big picture – if it is done in the right way, it is motivating for others and individuals can agree more specific goals in line with the business
- Performance management becomes a two-way process
- The manager is a part of the team, not apart from it, and is acknowledged as a working, contributing player

At Harvester Restaurants, the manager has become a

facilitator and encourages people towards self-management. Staff are empowered to do many things except decide whether they will be empowered!

Empowerment represents a fundamental shift for many organizations. The degree and speed of this shift depends on such factors as:

- Past history of the organization
- Industry or sector you are in
- Technology involved
- Competition
- Pace of change

EMPOWERMENT NEEDS TO START AT THE TOP

If you wish to devolve responsibility, the place you must start is at the top of the organization. It will be very difficult for employees to believe they truly have the power to make their own decisions if they perceive their managers have not changed their own behaviours. As one exasperated employee commented, *'Do you do what senior managers say you should or what you see people doing?'*

One organization in the catering business has evolved a way of enabling its employees to take responsibility. Each manager, starting from the most senior, has a dialogue with direct reports in order to identify:

- Areas of the job about which the employee would like to take decisions and where they need not refer directly to the boss for approval
- Areas of the job about which the employee may need to refer to the manager to sanction a decision
- No-go areas of corporate policy or procedure where employees do not have the power to decide

The discussion helps clarify expectations and allows the manager to agree with his or her team member the degree of empowerment they would like and what encouragement or support is needed to help that person in the job.

At Rover Group, managers are encouraged to let go of most of the tasks that they have held traditionally. Until the late 80s the company was very hierarchical. 'The only time you saw a manager was when he was firing someone or we were having a problem with production,' remembers one manager. Communication was top down and there was no opportunity to air grievances. Today, managers are locally based and there is no hierarchical behaviour based on status. Two-way communication is commonplace.

LEADERSHIP VALUES WHICH UNDERPIN EMPOWERMENT

Empowering leadership is underpinned by a consistent set of values, and people who live by them setting an example to others. The assumptions and values of empowering leadership are:

- Respect for people and valuing the strength of their different contributions
- Stress on the importance of open and honest communication
- Commitment to working co-operatively with others
- Recognition of the value of personal growth and development
- The importance of customer satisfaction, working to meet the needs of internal as well as external customers
- Awareness of improvement as a regular process in which everyone should be actively engaged

These values assist the organization to become more powerful and a better place to work for each individual.

Values come through in all kinds of actions. In the US, one of Kodak's manufacturing divisions created a set of values based around communications which led the way to an empowered culture. The importance of having open, honest and timely conversations is recognised by communications awards – to date there have been hundreds of winners.

HOW EMPOWERING IS YOUR LEADERSHIP STYLE?
Complete this questionnaire to find out!

	Always	Sometimes	Rarely
I encourage the members of my team to voice their opinions, even when these are critical of me.			
I allow my team to bypass me and go to my manager.			
I check back that my team understand their goals.			
My team shows energy and enthusiasm in what they do.			
I encourage my team to think beyond rules and procedures to anticipate and resolve problems.			
I make clear the expectations I have of my team.			
I share information on a regular basis with people inside and outside my team.			
My colleagues say that I don't hold on to rigid ideas or ways of doing things.			
I encourage my team members to talk about their career development and to take an active role in setting and meeting their development plans.			
I regularly give praise and recognition.			

Look at those items which you have scored 'sometimes' or 'rarely' and try to develop ways of changing these behaviours since they may block empowerment in others. Consider asking your team to complete this questionnaire about you and see if their perceptions match yours. Hold a discussion on the results.

EMPOWERING LEADERSHIP IN PRACTICE

Empowering leadership implies a willingness to devolve responsibility and that you help set the conditions in which other people can succeed. Here are some straightforward ways to do this:

- **Clarify expectations**

  Leaders should ensure that everyone develops a sound understanding of the requirements of their role. Team members need actively to offer input and seek clarification, and the leader's role is to encourage this to happen.

- **Appreciate everyone's contributions**

  Leaders should encourage an appreciative climate, *not* a blame culture. Give everyone the freedom to succeed rather than be overshadowed by the fear of failure.

- **Bring more people 'out of their organizational box'**

  Ensure people understand how they contribute to the success of the whole organization. Don't compartmentalize them and keep them in the dark about areas outside their 'box'.

- **Encourage everyone to speak out**

  Encourage everyone to voice their thoughts and be creative with new ideas, not just accept existing ways without active and constructive questioning.

A leadership model for empowerment

Empowering leadership needs to address four dimensions: **vision, reality, people** and **courage.** We will use these dimensions to explore more fully what empowering leadership entails.

1. Vision

The empowering leader:

- Sees the big picture and encourages an understanding in team members of how they fit into this
- Shares with the team new possibilities for the future
- Excites and motivates other people with a vision of what they are trying to achieve
- Encourages the team to devise ways of getting there

For example, Sun Life began the process of empowerment by asking groups of employees to draw their vision of the company of the future. This helped build a future which everyone could share.

2. Reality

Empowering leaders respond to and seek facts about what is really going on:

- They keep their feet firmly on the ground by regular 'reality checks'
- Do not get easily deluded or ignore warning signs
- They are aware of others, and also self-aware

For example, at Michelin Tyre the old foreman role has gone and with it the barriers that were imposed by progress chasing and inspection. Today, working relationships are closer and more open and therefore more in touch with reality.

3. People

The empowering leader is:

- Sensitive to people

- Ready to meet the needs of others and to do so in an ethical way which builds mutual trust and respect

For example, at the Benefits Agency structured feedback to senior managers has led to greater awareness of people issues. This feedback is reinforced by six-monthly personal development plans to promote change.

4. Courage
The empowering leader is:
- Ready to take the initiative
- Willing to take appropriate risks
- Not bounded by the way things have been done in the past or by undue fear of mistakes

For example, at Birmingham Midshires Building Society, the Chief Executive's bold vision of an empowered customer focused organization has inspired its employees to "turn an organization from the danger list to the prize winners' list in three years", as one analyst put it.

Together these four aspects of style and approach form a 'Leadership Diamond'. Like its gem namesake it is of considerable value, a durable source of strength and a means to cut through resistance and the toughest of barriers, to achieve results.

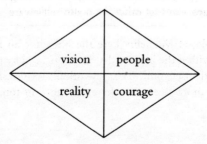

Good leadership is a well-balanced combination of these elements without major shortfalls in any one dimension or excessive emphasis on some aspects at the expense of others.

Sir Colin Marshall, former Chief Executive of British Airways, had the vision and courage to drive his organization forward into the 90s through empowerment and customer service, whilst recognizing the reality of the airline's competitive marketplace. He did so with an emphasis on people's contribution to the success of the organization.

But often leaders' styles can be unbalanced, with too much emphasis placed on some favourite approaches. The most helpful way for you as a leader to correct this is to **keep listening to feedback and setting personal development targets to improve your weaker areas.**

Truly empowering leaders need to behave in a way which emphasises all sides suggested by the Leadership Diamond and, through your good example, build leadership in others.

Anita Roddick of the Body Shop has this to say about empowering leadership:

(You have to look at leadership through the eyes of the followers and you have to live the message. What I have learned is that people become motivated when you guide them to the source of their own power and when you make heroes out of people who personify what you want to see in the organization.)

4

IMPLEMENTING EMPOWERMENT

You can expect implementation to take time and to have some unexpected consequences. You can also expect that there will be a lot of pressure to speed up the process and deliver quick results.

The process of implementing empowerment will lead to substantial change and upheaval in many organizations. Changing to an empowered environment often means a shift in roles and responsibilities as decision making is devolved down the line. This creates waves throughout the organization which needs managing through the process of implementation.

You therefore need to think through the implications before you begin – and do so again periodically during the change. We suggest you put this into a written plan of action with objectives, milestones and measurements. Because change is a people process, you should also think about providing information, encouragement and support to those involved.

THE EARLY STAGES OF IMPLEMENTATION

* **With your team develop concise, clear objectives which need to be achieved as a result of the changes.** Keep these objectives focused on the end result. It is very tempting to 'just get on with it' but you will have no reference point later on to measure progress. Continually refer back to your objectives – are they still being met? Do the objectives need to be modified? If they do need to be changed, are they still customer focused?

    The software development division within a computer

group held a series of workshops for all employees to examine the implementation of a new product strategy brought about by the merger of two organizations. Previously the two companies had operated independently.

Crucially, it involved participants from the two newly merged sites working together in equal numbers. Until then, change had produced mistrust between the sites, anxiety about the future and anger directed at what appeared to be secretive management. The workshops allowed these feelings to surface and a genuine dialogue to start.

- **Consider the effect on the customer.** Often internal preoccupations cause this to be overlooked until very late on. Keep in touch with your front line staff who often know most about the customer.

- **Do sufficient research to ensure the change is practicable and that your aims are realistic.** Birmingham Midshires Building Society set up over a dozen multi-function teams to investigate the practicalities of wide ranging changes.

- **Set up means to communicate the reasons for change clearly and vigorously so that everyone understands why changes are happening.** Kingston Hospital, who underwent many changes in the way it was structured in the early 90s, set up regular communications meetings so staff could discuss their concerns.

- **Assess who is affected – those who will benefit, those who will lose out, whether it be in status, job skills, responsibilities or power.** Look at the people involved in the processes you wish to change. Who are key people who could strongly affect the outcome? Who are the people whose support or input you need to achieve success? Remember these are not just people in your department. Involve them early.

At Liverpool's Children's Hospital a team of people with a very broad range of backgrounds – it included cleaners and consultants – set out to improve the service provided to out-patients. Its initiatives halved the length of the out-patient's visit and increased significantly the likelihood of a patient completing an examination in one visit.

- **Assess your own power and influence in the situation.** Are you likely to be able to carry the changes through? Whose help or support will you need? Who will you need to win over?

  e.g. You wish to establish a self-managing customer service team. You recognise that you need the support of the sales force to make the idea work. How do you convince this group of the benefits of your case? How soon do you involve them?

In promoting empowerment, remember that 'quick hits' help encourage others to take responsibility. Implement quick improvements straightaway. There is no need to wait for months for a full plan to be reviewed ready for implementation. As soon as you identify something that can help improve things, just do it. The newly appointed chairman of one company immediately removed the door to the executive area and put up a sign saying 'Everyone welcome'. The change was a dramatic signal of a new style of openness. Previously management had enclosed itself in a closed door isolation.

POINTERS IN PUTTING TOGETHER AN IMPLEMENTATION PLAN
Drawing up an implementation plan allows everyone

involved to know their responsibilities, time-scales and dependencies.

1. Training will be important for many people whose skills and knowledge need to be broadened. Plan ahead to set this up.

2. Discuss with your team what level of empowerment is:
- Ideal
- Acceptable
- Unacceptable

3. Listen to your team's suggestions on how you will measure success. When measures are agreed, let everyone in your team know these and the target results. Encourage the team members to set up mechanisms to inform everyone of the results so that they know how they are doing. At Harvester Restaurants, for example, each restaurant team decides its own goals and allocates responsibilities to help achieve these goals. Each team holds regular review seminars where results are shared and improvement actions defined.

4. Do not over-plan – allow the team some flexibility within agreed objectives. Expect the plan to need revision as time goes on.

5. Share responsibility for implementation into manageable and controllable pieces. Either:
- Spread the work over time within the team
- Ensure different people take responsibility for the success of each piece
- Or do both

It is often helpful to display the implementation plan in the form of a visual chart and to set aside a special area where people can inspect it, such as a team notice board.

SUGGESTIONS TO IMPLEMENT EMPOWERMENT SUCCESSFULLY

- **Consider piloting major change to iron out problems and reduce resistance and risk.**

  Eastern Group set out to improve the meter reading service it gave to customers, an area of particular customer dissatisfaction. In a pilot programme it consciously involved staff, who were previously seen as 'dyed-in-the-wool' conservative and resisting change, in the process of retraining and adopting new methods. The result surprised many people. The ideas were waiting to be tapped when the staff were treated with respect and the approach tailored to suit the group. The resulting pilot programme had a much more workable outcome and produced more motivated employees.

- **Give plenty of encouragement to successful change** – through reward, encouragement of enthusiasm and publicity. Be seen to be around and keep on top of how the affected people are getting on. Yardley of London put lots of publicity together to promote a new empowered team – posters, newsletters, distincitve uniforms. This raised the profile of the project and gave it status and importance.

- **Help people to adjust by providing coaching and training where appropriate.** Don't skimp on costs here, however tempting. Chapter 8 looks in more detail at training and development.

- **Be prepared to spend time with those particularly adversely affected by change.** Insurance group Cigna International (UK) carefully briefed those affected by major change well in advance and then modified training to take note of the issues which came up. Where there was resistance, people's fears and concerns were heard and acknowledged, sometimes over a period of months.

- **Don't be too ambitious in setting timescales** – people need time to adjust and in between, productivity may suffer. Too tight a timescale might lead to costly problems later on.

- **Maintain good systems of communication and information gathering inside and outside the company.** Birmingham Midshires Building Society has set up an internal communications group, with regular newsletter, monthly business progress briefings and two-way discussions with senior managers. It has adopted a rule that no information will be released externally until its staff are aware. Chapter 9 goes into more detail on communications.

- **Establish symbols of change** – new logos, names, slogans and special events help mark and symbolize change. Capture the reasons for change under these banners, with which people will readily identify. Birmingham Midshires use a symbol based on customer values called First Choice. For example, employees are given a First Choice Award for outstanding performance.

- **Tell your team colleagues about successes and others will be encouraged to follow this lead, thus making future change easier.** Software supplier SCO has successfully implemented large-scale improvements in its manufacturing and distribution activity which have led to substantial improvements in customer responsiveness and quality while, at the same, reducing stock levels and improving productivity. This has been achieved through involving every employee in examining with colleagues every aspect of processes and working practice. The active involvement of staff has been an example and stimulus for change elsewhere in the organization.

- **Tell customers about successful changes.** Some organizations send customers newsletters to keep them informed. Cigna used members of their 'change team' to take invited customers through the process of change which was underway.

DRAWING UP AN AGENDA FOR A TEAM EMPOWERMENT PLAN

Here are some questions which will help you formulate an agenda for a team empowerment action plan. These are best started at a facilitated team workshop where there is time to air views and speak freely. Many of the questions ask you to consider key aspects of change, especially ones not often given much open discussion.

Objectives
- Precisely what aspect of empowerment do we want changed, implemented and agreed?
- What measures will we use to indicate success?

Who is involved
- Who do we need to persuade? Change? Keep informed?
- What is their approach?
- What is their agenda – goals, interests, aims?
- What power does each of these groups or individuals hold? How do we deal with this?
- What is their likely response?
- Who is key to successful implementation?
- Who can make this fail?
- How do we minimise risk of failure?

Losses and Gains
- What are the benefits of these aspects of empowerment?

- What are the disadvantages, losses?
- What will we negotiate? What concessions can we make?

5

THE CUSTOMER AND EMPOWERMENT

Introduction

Empowerment is often introduced to help organizations create an environment which satisfies the customer. Customers' needs and concerns can be addressed and satisfied immediately. Staff are free to take opportunities to exceed customer expectations without referring upwards or fearing repercussions from their manager.

Empowerment is an important component of developing flexible and personal customer service. However, excellent service will not result simply by telling people they are empowered or taking out a layer of management to get close to the customer. Organizations need to adopt a systematic approach to empowered customer service, involving the individual in assessing the needs of customers. Best practice organizations also agree ways of measuring customer satisfaction, and again, full involvement of staff in this process is essential for commitment and quality outcomes.

HOW DOES THE CUSTOMER BENEFIT FROM EMPOWERMENT?

In an empowered organization individuals recognise the important part they play in delivering service to the customer. They have the authority and flexibility to ensure they deliver service to a high standard. An empowered organization, therefore, is easy for the customer to do business with – its entire manner of doing business is geared towards the needs of the customer.

Home banking services company First Direct has revolutionized the way service is provided in the domestic financial sector. The company has a philosophy of empowered customer service. It regularly surveys customers to establish their satisfaction with current service levels and their future requirements, and then communicates this information to employees. It has consciously broken down potential internal barriers to good communication by creating a working environment where everyone is known on a first name basis and works together in open-plan offices.

Empowered contributors recognize that customer service means exceeding the expectations of their customers. In an empowered company, people share responsibility for problems and are proactive in their response to the customer.

The customer recognizes empowerment – service providers' attitudes are positive and people go out of their way to help.

Empowerment, therefore, will be visible to the customer through people's *behaviours,* their *attitudes* and the *values* that underlie them. In the empowered organization it isn't internal policies or rules which are important, it is *customer satisfaction.*

The US restaurant chain Taco Bell underwent transformation from a rule-bound, centralized company to one where the customer is at the heart of every decision. Local branches are given the authority to work autonomously within the framework of the brand. This change of focus has meant that employees are now perceived from the outside to be more customer-orientated and levels of service have risen.

At the Automobile Association, customer interfacing staff are empowered to deal with members' complaints and difficulties in the best way they see fit. If, for example, a customer experiencing a delay in the arrival of a patrol is a woman on her own, the call operator may suggest that she has a meal in the nearest cafe or restaurant at the AA's expense. The organization has supported empowered employees to use their discretion via a series of training events and through the coaching role played by team supervisors.

HOW DOES AN ORGANIZATION CREATE A CUSTOMER FOCUS THROUGH EMPOWERMENT?

One of the hardest aspects of creating an empowered environment is engendering in employees a belief and confidence that they have freedom in the way they do things.

Empowerment and customer focus don't just appear overnight once the management has committed to the process. In a company manufacturing electrical equipment, employees had attended a series of special meetings at the request of their MD. He declared that they were now empowered to serve the customer in the way they best saw fit.

Following the meeting, one employee decided that stock levels on certain components always caused delays to customers. It would be better to hold more of these items in stock. Another employee, a service engineer, felt that the amount of time allocated for each customer visit was too short. He decided to extend the length of each visit.

Both employees were disappointed and resentful to have their actions questioned by their manager and decisions changed in both cases. The company directors had not put into place sufficient pre-planning and co-ordination to ensure that discretion on ideas for service improvement was defined and supported by all involved. They had failed to recognize the uphill task to gain buy-in methods to establish customer needs. They were also naive in failing to see the knock-on effects on the rest of the organization.

RECOGNIZING THE NEEDS OF THE CUSTOMER

Front line staff hold a wealth of information on their customers and are the people in the organization who are closest to customers' needs. In order to create a customer focus through empowerment it is essential to canvass staff's views on what should change and why.

A national fashion retailer was very concerned to improve its sales. It held focus groups with its shop staff, who suggested better fitting rooms and a seating area with coffee to create a more congenial atmosphere. The suggestions were taken up and customers have welcomed the changes.

External customer surveys

Many empowered organizations involve their staff actively in gathering and reviewing customer feedback. Employees are more likely to take ownership of the information gathered from customers if they have a greater insight into customers' perceptions.

Surveys can take many forms – focus groups or face-to-face discussions, comment cards, postal or telephone surveys. The key is to listen to customers and then to use their comments to develop a plan of action for improvement with the involvement of employees.

At Mercedes-Benz, six-monthly postal surveys provide an index of customer satisfaction. These surveys are supplemented in certain dealerships by the use of telephone interviews. Customers who visit the showroom or who use the service or repair centre are contacted a few days after their visit to ascertain how satisfied they were with the service and to identify areas of improvement. The information is then fed back to staff and joint actions agreed between a manager and his or her team members.

Many organizations use feedback to develop charters and set standards for the delivery of excellent customer service.

Staff adopt such charter standards most readily when they are empowered to develop them. A high street retailer recently set up groups of employees from across the company to develop a set of service standards. Using information gathered on what was significant to the customer, the teams developed measurable and achievable standards which are now used as agreed bench-marks to conduct shop and individual performance reviews.

Recognizing the needs of the internal customer

A key aspect of empowerment is *mutual accountability*. Many organizations promote the concept of the internal customer by holding awareness sessions and discussion groups with parts of the company who provide a service to each other. It is also useful to set up internal service improvement groups with volunteer employees from all parts of the organization. These groups can come up with suggestions on ways to get smarter and to work together more effectively.

The quality of service which front line staff deliver is the product not only of individuals' personal skills, attitudes and behaviour, but also the skills, attitudes and behaviour of other stakeholders in the service delivery process.

The end product that reaches the customer, be it a product or service, therefore, is the sum of all the links in the chain leading to the customer. To take the example of the Customer Services department of a fast moving consumer goods company, there are many links to the internal customer chain:

To provide an excellent service to the external customer, members of the customer service team are dependent upon many other parts of the business. One customer service group took the initiative to work with the marketing department to ensure customer queries were not left unanswered for days. Until then, the marketing function had not appreciated the urgency of these queries and this lack of understanding was reinforced by the geographical separation of the two departments.

Process improvements and process redesign initiatives often help improve internal service quality. At the National & Provincial Building Society, the introduction of empowerment has been accompanied by business process re-engineering. The management structure has been flattened and the business is now centred around processes.

Employees take on one of four roles: process leaders, implementation managers, team leaders or players. This exercise has brought about much greater awareness of other functions by employees.

6

EMPOWERMENT THROUGH TEAMWORK

Effective teamwork gives strength to an empowered climate. In the past, work teams tended to be less important to business success and many organizations still live with this legacy. In today's fast changing environment people need to work closely with others, even though individually they may be empowered. A shared sense of collective responsibility through teamwork adds real strength to an organization. Individuals can feel a sense of belonging and recognition and this can spur them on to overcome problems and push to meet stretching goals.

Teamwork can be hard work for many people more used to working on their own, particularly in the early stages of the development of a team. Managers and team leaders need to be very supportive, and in many cases they themselves need a lot of support to be sufficiently behind the idea. However, a team-based organization is on a clear route to empowerment, so careful and regular nurturing will pay off handsomely until it becomes a way of life.

You must pay attention to all aspects of the supporting environment – the history and culture, systems and rewards. Learning to work together produces dividends, but there is a cost in getting there which many organizations have found daunting. For those who stick the course, there are considerable rewards.

THE IMPETUS TO BRING TEAMWORKING AND EMPOWERMENT TOGETHER

Many of the drivers for change give impetus to increased teamwork:

• Rapid or frequent organizational changes mean groups

are more regularly forming and disbanding. Nissan UK instituted major changes in 1994. To cement this it held fifty team events to quickly build new relationships for 20,000 people. Some pundits predict organizations will soon be composed entirely of 'virtual teams' – groups of people who come together to carry out specific tasks and so form, disband and reform regularly, and who network with few restrictions caused by hierarchies or boundaries.

• Increased spans of authority for many managers have forced them to let go of their traditional control and allow greater team self-direction.

• The ability to share new ideas and information quickly is becoming paramount as competitive pressures demand originality, higher standards and enhanced output.

• As many organizations experience the thrust to do more with less, the benefits of empowered teamwork grow more attractive:

1. The ability to make more than the sum of the parts.

2. To communicate rapidly to solve problems and take initiatives.

3. To build a shared loyalty, motivation and identity.

• Teams provide employees with a sense of belonging and support which gives individuals the confidence to take on more responsibilities and make decisions affecting their workplace.

In response to a need to become more globally competitive, Zeneca Agrochemicals, based in Yalding, replaced functional departments with cross functional teams based on product families of fifteen people. Continuous improvement using team ideas has led to a 13 percent productivity increase in the first year of operation. Teams are now encouraged to take ownership of their own problems, not leave them to specialists. Each team maintains its own equipment, and has responsibility for the total process for its product group, from bulk materials storage to finished goods warehousing. Team leaders have taken on wider responsibilities, are closer to their teams and are less likely to be the sole expert that people turn to. Communication is now much improved with team meetings at least once a week.

WHAT IS AN EMPOWERED TEAM?

The term 'empowered team' needs a clear definition. One definition which we find helpful is:

(A small number of people with complementary skills who are committed to a common purpose, performance goals and approach for which they hold themselves mutually accountable.)

It is this mutual accountability which singles out the empowered team. Empowered teams are likely to emerge from groups of three to ten people – some would say eight maximum. These teams have built a shared sense of direction even though they often have different perspectives, skills and contributions. This bond is strong enough to feel a sense of ownership for team issues and for individuals to put themselves out to support other team members.

The heart of an empowered organization is frequently the network of teams who work together daily, on the shop floor, in the quality department, in the offices. There are also teams formed in different contexts and with rather different characteristics, for example: project teams, improvement teams, cross-functional problem solving teams. We believe that if you get regular teams to work well, multi-functional teams will also work effectively.

WHAT MAKES AN EMPOWERED TEAM PERFORM WELL?

- Leadership which gives a clear lead and example to others – but is prepared to work through the team, not insist on one-way decision making. At Nissan UK great stress is placed on the role of the first-line team leader to coach and build a team.

- Sense of purpose – keeping a constant eye on where you want to go as a team and having the mechanisms in place to adjust course, also ensuring measurements are explicit against defined and agreed objectives. These are determined by the team, not imposed on them.

- Making use of the different team members' complementary skills – people listen to each other and all useful contributions can be drawn out.

- Team leaders in particular but also team members encourage and coach others and share information.

- An open and supportive culture where people have the self-confidence to know that mistakes can occur if you take necessary risks, but that the individual or the team will not be scapegoated. At Michelin Tyre it took time to build trust and confidence in self-directed teams, with the freedom to make some mistakes at first.

- Regular contact – the more people work in isolation or apart, the more likely it is that misunderstandings are to arise. Nissan UK teams meet every day for five minute communication sessions.

- Individuals are prepared to take a collective stance and

recognize and support a common view.

- Meetings of such groups are focused and disciplined, but there is time enough to hear people and resolve tensions and get agreement to actions.

Domestic heating company Baxi has based its whole organization around team working to become more customer responsive, with better communications and cost control. Two key factors in the success of its empowered teams are heavy investment in training and development, coupled with a culture and systems which support empowered teams.

SELF-DIRECTED TEAMS

Empowerment in teamwork is exemplified by the self-directed team which is beginning to be established in some UK organizations. The key component is that there is no visible day-to-day controlling manager; *management responsibilities are devolved to team members who each perform managerial tasks in addition to their functional roles.* Recruitment, work scheduling, training, output and performance management are all the team's responsibility. When problems arise it is the team's job to understand and solve issues whether they are to do with getting the job done or with relationships inside and outside the team.

In the UK self-managing teams can be found within a number of well-known organizations such as Rank Xerox and Sun Alliance. Team members often perform discrete functions over and above their task roles which allow them to operate as a complete unit and to take all decisions affecting their work area.

Experience shows that creating and sustaining self-governing teams is not easy. Harvester Restaurants believes clear accountabilities are a key feature of success. It has drawn up this list of responsibilities for its teams:

WHAT	WHO
Vision	Team Manager
How implemented	Teams
Monitoring	Coach
Progress reports, recognition	Team Manager

How to build a self-directed work team

Experience of self-directed teams suggests that they benefit from:

1. Clearly understood team purpose and responsibilities.
2. Knowing what are the boundaries of authority and decision making.
3. Understanding of individual roles within the team.
4. Ground rules which are explicit, understood, generated and owned by all team members. For example, one team of trainers set out the following ways of working together which it displays prominently in the trainers' room:

- communicate with each other
- don't hide difficulties
- share
- help each other out
- keep workspace tidy

What are the signs of a self-directed team?

- wholehearted ownership of all aspects of the process
- work is self-controlled, from planning and budgeting to completion
- conflicts are resolved in the team
- continuous improvement is in evidence
- team members take responsibility for development and training
- budget responsibility is accepted
- recognition and reward are determined with input from the whole team

A PROGRESSIVE APPROACH TO INTRODUCTION

Some organizations have found it helpful to adopt a phased approach to move from a traditional to an empowered self-managed team.

LEVEL 1

Getting underway. The team leader is held accountable for all key aspects of the team's performance. As the team builds up confidence, team members start to accept accountability, particularly for routine and short-term issues. Objectives are set by the team leader and training needs are identified by him or her. The budget is set outside the team but day-to-day management of expenses may be controlled in the team.

LEVEL 2

Moving forward. The team leader is still taking a managing role, with responsibility for some longer-term or contentious issues, but medium-term and routine issues are now handled in the group. Objectives are set by the team but are reviewed with the leader. Training is identified jointly between team members and the team leader. Budget planning and monitoring becomes a joint activity. Pay may contain an element which is based on team performance. People often describe this phase as the most challenging for all concerned – for the team leader in handing over responsibilities and adopting a new style, and for the team member in picking up new skills and testing them out.

LEVEL 3

Success. Team members take responsibility for all issues, short and long-term. They set their own objectives and output measures after discussion. Training is identified by team members who also accept responsibility for setting and discharging aspects of company-wide development plans. Just as they contribute to the business plan, the team is responsible for setting and managing its own budgets.

Team-based reward and recognition systems are in place. The team leader either becomes a coach and facilitator or may be eliminated entirely. Often the functions previously carried out by a human resources department, such as discipline, setting pay, recruitment and selection, are taken over by the team. Also the same is true with the finance function since members of all service functions now become advisors, not police.

This process of development may take up to two years to achieve. On the way, team members will need to acquire new skills and more broadly based knowledge than they had before.

Systems to support empowered teams
The empowered team needs appropriate systems which work to buttress the change:

* **Regular and systematic communication systems.** (see Chapter 9 on Communications)

* **Reward and recognition** – the team needs to consider ways to reward the whole team as well as individual performance. Frizzell Financial Services now pays performance bonuses on a team basis rather than purely to individuals. (see Chapter 7 for more information on reward and recognition)

* **Appraisal and feedback** – the team needs to ensure regular balanced feedback is given to encourage a blame-free supportive learning environment. Rank Xerox UK customer services division encourages team feedback on each other's work to promote openness in discussing customer issues and a greater sense of responsibility. (see Chapter 7)

* **Training and development** – team members need to encourage sharing of learning and undertake self-

directed development such as self study. Induction training is a vital way of developing the values and skills required in the team. Systems need to be in place and supported to ensure it is done well. Kingston Hospital has defined core competencies for its cross-functional care teams and encourages wider learning beyond this. (see Chapter 8 for a broader examination of training and development)

Steps in forming a new empowered team
From the word 'go':

- Define the purpose and work together to agree roles for each other within that overall purpose.

- Recruit with the whole team in mind – don't just select on individual experience and skills. Look for potential to multi-skill.

- Get off to a good start by holding an early team-building event to get to know each other. At this meeting consider not just the *what* (i.e. what needs to be achieved) but also the *how* (i.e. how are we going to work together, what is important to us, what happens if we disagree). Expect to hold such meetings regularly, say every two or three months.

- Review and renew your thinking and plans regularly. A traditional team can become a bit like an ocean liner – once it has started in one direction, changing course can be hard. An empowered team will often avoid this problem because continuous improvement is easier and more natural. Make sure you look regularly at the need for changes to your plans.

- Agree to meet regularly and stick to it. Don't fall into the trap of being too busy to meet together. By meeting together often, get into the habit of using team members as a resource to solve issues and support each other when the going gets tough.

Empowered team work in action – a case study

Yardley of London

This long established UK based world-wide manufacturer of cosmetics and perfumes with over six hundred employees had considerable problems of poor profitability and delivery, low productivity and morale.

The first stage in renewal was dramatic – the redundancy of six of the old production supervisors. The management felt the autocratic, hierarchical supervisors had to change or leave the organization. Many simply did not fit the new culture of a facilitating, coaching, open style team leader. To reinforce this coaching role, the power of discipline was taken away from the new leaders, thus building closer relationships with employees free from the old fears of hire and fire. Team leaders were given support through training in leadership, team and quality improvement skills.

A pilot production team enthusiastically attacked improvement projects it had defined itself. At first this surprised management, who realised they had under-estimated the capabilities of the individuals and the power of a newly motivated team to drive change forward. Team pride was enhanced by new facilities and equipment as well as extensive training, for example the team had to learn how to work together effectively as an empowered group.

The success of the first empowered team encouraged the company to extend the programme to other production areas. Today, business is growing in sales and profitability and quality is noticeably stronger.

7

MANAGING PERFORMANCE

Introduction
Increasing attention is being paid to performance management as organizations have got leaner and demand more focused effort from their staff. An empowering approach offers much greater opportunities for successful joint management of performance and increased productivity.

Performance management is one lever in achieving empowerment which links to business goals. We recommend to you a high degree of employee involvement in this area, from design through to review, recognition and reward. Performance management should stress development, not one-way judgement by managers.

The essence of effective reward, recognition and incentive schemes should be *fairness* – recognizing targeted behaviour in the right staff, at the right time and for the right reasons.

Empowered organizations strive to create an environment which recognizes the value of regular positive feedback. *'Thank you, well done'* should be a regular feature of an empowered culture, from colleagues as well as managers.

Performance management defined

The Performance Management Cycle:

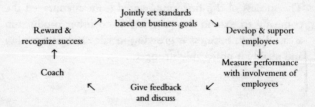

Performance management is a management approach which allows employees to link business goals with their own goals and responsibilities. As the diagram shows it involves an integrated process of supporting business objectives by helping individuals set agreed relevant objectives and standards of performance. In an empowered environment, performance management helps provide a framework and direction for employees and allows the manager to identify the support he or she must provide. With coaching, development and reward, improved performance is possible so that employees consistently know:

- what is expected of them
- how they are doing
- what they need to do next
- what support they will receive

ICL has modified its performance management system to move away from highly controlled structures and hierarchical appraisals. Today it stresses personal ownership, career management and self-managed learning. It has sent booklets to all employees on how to manage their careers. It has established self-managing learning groups where people can share their development plans and support each other. In this way it is demonstrating a vision of performance management as a tool for the learning organization.

Many of the conditions which facilitate empowerment also help the success of performance management:

- Clear and open objectives which are consistent and equitable in the way they are set and reviewed.
- A 'no blame' culture, so people feel free to talk about weaknesses and accept criticisms, provided these are given sensitively and with respect.
- Goals are jointly set by the manager and the individual and are monitored so that they are realistic and attainable.

- Managers listen carefully to employees (and vice versa) and there is open and regular face-to-face discussion, including the freedom to criticize the actions of managers.
- There is a forward-looking results orientation, not a backward-looking culture which puts the blame on individuals.
- Action plans are agreed, with time-scales and measures to show how much progress is being made.
- Success is recognized and rewarded, financially and otherwise.
- Reward mechanisms are seen to be fair and open.
- Employees have participated in the design of the whole process.

This list strongly suggests that empowering performance management will be effective where relationships are working well. Organizations who have empowered performance management have found success is a lot less dependent on the elegance of paperwork or ingenuity of systems, though of course careful design of the performance management process provides a framework.

The National & Provincial Building Society has developed a set of thirty-two competencies, eight of which serve as 'action points' for an individual's work. Each person's performance is reviewed by their colleagues, team leader and fellow team members against their competencies. Pay is also determined by the level of competence. The organization has also moved to a system of flexible benefits whereby employees are given the choice of a range of remuneration benefits.

At NatWest Group the performance management process starts with and integrates into the group vision. Each business and support sector is encouraged to create its own vision which links and contributes to the corporate vision. Strategic goals are set at group level, while at unit level teams develop business goals and action plans to help deliver the strategic goals. Local goals focus on customer service, business services, quality and people and business efficiency.

Like some other organizations who are encouraging empowerment, the bank has developed a set of competencies and behaviours that apply to each job. The competencies are grouped together to form job profiles. For example, in customer service support roles these are:

- Information gathering
- Problem solving
- Customer service
- Communication skills
- Attention to detail
- Process operation

Competencies set out the behaviours the individuals are expected to demonstrate in order to do their job effectively. They provide a clear and transparent basis of measurement of performance through the assessment of the contribution an individual has made to the business. The employees know their level of performance and how to extend this.

CONDITIONS FOR SUCCESS

Appraisal schemes have traditionally been at the centre of performance management systems yet most companies have a poor track record in this respect. An empowered culture needs to be supported by a system which everyone owns. In the past, managers and employees alike have been reluctant to own appraisal schemes and the only enthusiasm seems to have come from HQ or personnel departments. *So how is performance management likely to succeed in an empowered environment? What are the conditions which generate success of a pay system?* Many pay schemes have been designed to increase performance, often with disappointing results. The key conditions of success are:

1. Participation in the design

Participation in the design and administration process for a performance management system, including reward systems, can make all the difference to its effectiveness. This will probably mean a break with the past since very few organizations have been able to let go of notions of 'management's right to manage' in this area, and keep the whole thing hush-hush.

At South Somerset District Council unit managers participated in brainstorming sessions to determine a set of management competencies against which performance is measured.

2. What you communicate

Employees are often left to themselves to find out about the aims and mechanisms of performance and pay systems. The effect is that they may exaggerate inequalities and perceptions of unfairness. Regular open communication is vital; for example, what is the scheme aiming to achieve? How does it operate? What are the pay ranges? How does one's salary fit into other job groups? What is the organization paying in relation to the market? What training is available to promote advancement? How is selection for courses made?

Too often performance management remains focused on past behaviours rather than future development and career plans. An engineering organization has instigated a process for career development discussion between the manager and individual. These are held separately from appraisal and are used to heighten awareness and discuss career development, without the constraints of assessment. It is hoped that this process will help to clarify what managers expect of the individual and what he or she can expect of management.

It will allow the person to draw up realistic development plans with the respective parts owned by all those involved.

3. How you gather feedback on performance

Traditionally, performance review has been a one-way discussion between manager and subordinate based on the manager's assessment of the individual's past performance. In an empowered environment, feedback becomes a more open process with input gathered from a variety of sources rather than just the manager. Many organizations now use 360 degree feedback – feedback on performance from all levels of employees with whom the individual has contact to help gain a better picture of an individual's strengths and weaknesses. At Motorola, for example, managers receive feedback from their boss, team peers and team subordinates across a spectrum of skill areas. This helps individuals create personal development plans which are reviewed regularly and are also linked to performance-related pay.

To ensure the effectiveness of 360 degree feedback:

- Keep the process straightforward, usually with a structured questionnaire
- Ensure the questionnaire encourages a balanced approach, with positive comment as well as negative
- Guarantee confidentiality

4. Training which managers and employees receive

Performance management systems are only as good as the behaviour of the people who operate them. Not only managers but all employees should be trained in the process of performance management and how to get the most from them. The areas of training for managers will be, typically:

- setting jointly agreed objectives
- carrying out two-way performance discussions
- giving specific feedback
- discussion of performance shortfalls
- coaching and developing staff
- operation of reward and recognition systems
- when and how to review performance

Training for individual contributors will cover some of this ground but will concentrate on the purpose of the scheme, for example: the role employees play in its success, receiving feedback constructively, giving feedback and setting objectives.

At Courtaulds the word 'appraisal' is no longer used. Managers have been given training in coaching and developing their staff through regularly reviewing performance. This is generating a more open climate and increased frequency of communication between managers and their teams.

In an empowered environment, performance review is a regular event. It becomes part of the day-to-day relationship between the manager and the team. It focuses on development and improvement, rather than looking out for mistakes. In addition, best practice organizations place considerable responsibility for development with the individual, so the review process is jointly owned rather than something which is 'done to' the individual.

Performance management checklist
Rate how your current performance management system meets the needs of an empowered culture on a scale of 1 to 5 where 1 = *does not meet the needs,* and 5 = *fully meets the needs*.

		1	2	3	4	5
1.	Continuous connection between business goals and personal performance.					
2.	Team and individual contributions are recognized and acknowledged.					
3.	Jointly agreed development plans are prepared to ensure performance improvement.					
4.	Scheme reflects needs of all groups of employees.					
5.	Allows for meeting future needs as well as present.					
6.	Performance management, reward and recognition are supportive of an empowered culture and do not conflict with each other.					
7.	Simple to understand and manage.					

Now total your score. If you score twenty or below, your performance management system may well need reviewing to meet the needs of an empowered environment.

Motivation and reward

What makes people work well and energetically and what processes and strategies will help achieve this aim in an empowered way? The starting point for managers should be 'don't assume!'

Involving your employees in the design of payment schemes ensures that there is real understanding of employee needs and will ensure greater ownership. The first step is to ask employees what motivates them and why. This can be done either on an individual or team basis, using attitude surveys, focus groups or through cross-functional task groups.

A company in the financial services industry recently undertook an attitude survey together with focus groups at the beginning of a customer service programme to establish what motivated its employees. The organization is very results-driven and expected that employees would identify cash incentives as a prime motivator. Instead, the strong response was 'recognition for a job well done.' 'Catching people getting it right' was not part of the culture of the organization. The survey prompted senior managers to re-evaluate the way things were done. The consequence was the instigation of a culture change programme resulting in a fundamental rethink of company values. Many leading practitioners of empowerment recognize the importance of tracking employee satisfaction. They assess the motivation of their workforce in the same way as they assess customer satisfaction. Companies such as Rank Xerox and Avis regularly conduct surveys to identify satisfaction levels.

Incentives and rewards
The old proverb 'what gets measured gets done' can also be interpreted as 'what gets rewarded gets attention'.

Payment for achievement of objectives can have a powerful impact on getting target tasks achieved, though you need to take care that other, non-targeted areas do not suffer and that competition between groups or employees does not become destructive. A large retailer introduced a bonus scheme for all its front line staff. This caused resentment amongst head office and support staff who were not included in the programme.

If you are considering devising incentive schemes you should consider carefully whether to reward teams or individuals. Rewarding teams encourages collaboration and achievement of team goals, for example. It can, however, be said to discourage recognition of individual effort.

Also check that the introduction of a scheme is appropriate. British Telecom introduced an internal award scheme entitled 'Living our Values'. Unfortunately, this was at a time of large-scale redundancies and the reaction of some staff to the scheme was, naturally, somewhat negative.

Whatever the criteria for the award they must be seen to be a credible basis for decisions. Citroen consulted both its employees and its customers in order to establish the criteria for a 'customer-driven award scheme' for forecourt staff and their managers.

Building a climate of personal recognition and non-monetary reward

Empowerment can be encouraged through recognition and rewarding people in symbolic ways. Non-monetary rewards can have a very positive effect on motivation. These can range from a thank you letter, to a bunch of flowers or a meal out. A 'thank you' or 'well done' timed near to the event and meant sincerely may give more value to the receiver than cash or tokens.

People can be recognized in different ways. Depending on the culture of the organization, 'employee of the month' schemes can prove motivational. Employees are invited to nominate the person whom they believe should receive an award. One software company has successfully devised and implemented a scheme whereby each quarter employees nominate their colleagues from other parts of the company who have provided outstanding service to help them achieve their own goals.

A group of high street opticians has devised a 'thank you' and 'well done' scheme to recognize how well employees support each other. The scheme has been included as part of the internal measurement process. Each department counts the numbers of thank you cards received per quarter and these then form part of the criteria for internal awards.

A well-known soup manufacturer has produced and made special gold soup cans so that departments can award these to any team member for exceptional effort.

8

TRAINING AND DEVELOPMENT

Introduction

There has been a sharp increase in the importance attached to employee training as a means to support the transformation to an empowered organization. Many organizations who seek empowerment put considerable emphasis on coaching and developing their employees as a vehicle of change.

They see training and development as vital ingredients to putting the process of empowerment into action. All the organizations we have talked to recognized that employees cannot be expected to take responsibility for decisions affecting their jobs unless they feel confident they have the skills and knowledge to do so.

Our experience suggests major investment in training is called for as part of successful empowerment. Training and development techniques which encourage empowerment reflect a wide variety of approaches, no simple technique is likely to be *the* answer.

A long term commitment

There are no quick solutions to fostering empowerment through training. Avis in the UK has spent over ten years developing an empowered customer-driven culture. British Airways, who instigated a major training-led culture change programme to create a customer focus during the 80s, emphasizes that the journey to excellence is never-ending. In the 90s it recognizes that although it has come far, it needs to keep on training year after year as the requirement for change and improvement is constantly rising.

The only approach which will lay the foundations for

success is based on a thorough and continuous cycle of development involving a variety of types of training and coaching techniques:

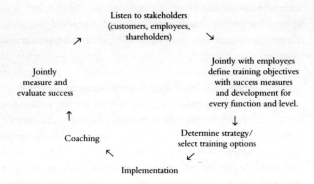

Listen to stakeholders (customers, employees, shareholders)

Jointly with employees define training objectives with success measures and development for every function and level.

Jointly measure and evaluate success

Coaching

Determine strategy/ select training options

Implementation

DEFINING TRAINING AND DEVELOPMENT OBJECTIVES

There are various methods for defining training and development objectives in an empowering way, all of which can involve employees actively in the process.

- gaining customer feedback
- asking employees for their views and needs
- peer group assessment
- individual self-assessment

An organization's prime focus should be to meet the needs of its stakeholders and customers and employees should get particular attention. Customer feedback is vital to help identify how well employees are matching customer expectations. Training and development solutions can then be designed to meet these needs.

P & O European Ferries conducted an extensive survey to determine in what way it needed to respond to changing customer needs and encourage greater empowerment. Its training strategy was built around the results of the survey. To keep training focused on changing business needs it now holds monthly customer focus groups. Initially it made the mistake of failing to involve all groups of employees sufficiently in its customer programme and the result was somewhat patchy. Later it realized and corrected this deficiency to ensure that everyone felt part of the process of change.

In 1995 Walsall Council took a bold decision to define its vision and strategy for change. It invited a wide cross-section of 300 employees and members of the community to a two-day event to agree a set of priorities. The outcome was an implementation plan which has been turned into focused development plans, with an energised and inspired workforce embarking on quality improvement initiatives.

THE ROLE OF MANAGEMENT

Training and development will only be effective if managers play an active part because they are visible role models and are so important in encouraging changes and coaching employees. A training strategy which aims to encourage empowerment will not become part of an organization's life if managers resist and fail to believe in it or act by its principles. It is important to hold managers accountable for developing their staff in new ways – at every level of the organization.

Organizations seeking true empowerment must identify ways to:

- Assist managers to recognize the role they can play in promoting a *learning culture*.
- Encourage them to act as coaches to their staff.
- Involve them in the training and development process from initial planning through to delivery and execution.

- Emphasize that everyone needs to assist each other.

At Michelin Tyre managers played a key role in analysing training needs and carrying out training. To support the new self-managed decision making, managers drew up detailed team operating procedures and assisted in the introduction of comprehensive self-learning packages. This helped to create a workforce which would take decisions with the requisite knowledge and consistent approach, encouraged by managers.

THE LEARNING ORGANIZATION
In the empowered organization greater ownership of training and development is placed on the individual. Many companies now encourage staff, in discussion with their manager, to create their own personal development plans. Hewlett-Packard in the UK has issued all its employees with a lifelong learning record to promote personal responsibility for development. It sends quite the wrong message if the responsibility for the training and development of employees rests solely with the manager or the training department. The emphasis in the empowered organization is on *continuous development* which takes place in and out of the workplace using techniques which best suit the individual's learning style. More and more organizations are allowing employees to undertake learning in any chosen area, as pioneered on a large scale by the Rover Group.

How receptive is your organization to learning?
To be successful, an organization needs every employee to keep on learning. This checklist helps you to assess how receptive your organization is to learning new things. For each pair of statements, consider your organization and tick the number which best corresponds to your views.

	1	2	3	4	5	
Most people in my organization agree that when things are working well it's best to leave them as they are						Even when things appear to be working well, many people find ways to improve them
People rather resent change and learning new things						There is a general atmosphere of wanting to learn new things
There are many people who like to get their own ideas across						You can expect most people to listen first to other people's ideas before they put forward their own
I feel uncomfortable asking for help in solving a problem						I frequently ask for help when I need to solve a problem
The motto round here is 'stick to what we know will work' and not risk things going wrong						I am encouraged to take a risk on new ideas even for things that I know work well now
Many people agree that their learning days are over						We are encouraged to adopt the philosophy that you're never too old or experienced to learn
We don't have time to find out what other organizations and people are doing to tackle our sort of work						We take time to look around at what others are doing
I can't remember the last time I learnt something new						I have learnt something new this week
When we have a problem we solve it in the same way as we have done in the past						We like to look into new ways of solving problems
We are encouraged to be specialists, to solve our own problems						Generally, people are willing to listen to others to help solve a problem

Now total your score. If your score totalled 35 or more, your organization adopts a positive approach to learning. If you scored below this, think how your organization could become more receptive to learning. It is difficult to encourage people to learn unless there is a positive approach to learning and training, so what example can you set to help build a more helpful and encouraging approach?

You might consider giving this questionnaire to your team and encouraging a discussion on the general results and how you could create a stronger learning environment.

COACHING

As companies go down the path of empowerment, greater awareness is often generated of the need for continuous self-improvement. Hence managers in empowered organizations should start to adopt a facilitative role in helping their staff to develop. This involves encouraging employees in a supportive and encouraging way to:

- assess where they are now in terms of skills and where they need to be
- set targets for their development
- select the most appropriate development methods
- review their progress and set future targets

Pharmaceuticals giant Glaxo Wellcome has recently undergone a radical change process and many teams have created the role of 'team coach' to help facilitate greater learning within the team.

Points for effective coaching

There are four points that coaches should watch out for when helping individuals to develop, based on extensive research into successful coaching of sales staff:

- Put the person at their ease – employees may feel self-conscious and therefore less receptive to what the coach has to say if they are defensive because they feel under criticism or made to feel inadequate.
- Don't assume your way is the only way – ask

questions to ascertain the other person's perspective and approach.

- Help the person focus on one improvement area at a time – don't overload the person with too many points at once.
- Help the person to set specific goals to practise the new skills and follow them up – don't assume that once is enough for a new skill to take root.

Narrow, 'sheep-dip' training is not enough

A universal or 'sheep–dip' approach to training will not be sufficient to empower. Organizations wishing to empower should adopt a holistic approach to training and development. This involves taking a wide-ranging approach: how will the training affect the organization and vice versa? What impact will it have on the team? What individual characteristics and preferences need to be taken into account? Training needs to consider three overlapping areas:

You can help individuals to become empowered by taking account of the **organizational** context in which individuals are to be developed as well as **individual** and **team** needs. You can usefully introduce ways of promoting continuous improvement, such as cross-functional improvement teams, focus groups and suggestion schemes.

One national hotel group recognizes this broad span of influences in conducting organizational and service reviews of each part of its business. The reviews focus on finance, culture, structure and people capabilities in order to measure how well the business is working. The information for them is based on simple focused self-assessments by the business units. The reviews have promoted greater individual accountability and involvement and have led to targeted development plans.

Healthcare organization BUPA has instituted a change programme to help it continue to be successful in a fiercely competitive market. It has launched its programme with a frank admission that the outcome of some of its previous 'top down' initiatives was disappointing and that it has learned from past mistakes. This time it has ensured that there is:

- involvement which is actively encouraged
- visible and involved top management support
- a clearly defined and communicated process and rationale for change, set in the context of a vision of the business
- demonstrable changes and improvements

Prudential Assurance set out to improve the way it handled customer complaints. It started off by a thorough analysis of two questions:

- What culture do we want to build?
- How do the existing processes and procedures fit?

It involved its employees in answering the questions. In this way it built a highly successful plan to train and develop effectively.

Because working together as a team frequently increases an individual's ability to deliver results, empowered organizations often emphasise the value of training as a whole team. (see Chapter 6 on teamwork)

Multi-skilling and a wider range of knowledge become a key focus for training individuals and teams. This training may cover:

- business awareness
- skills in handling differences and appreciating diversity
- meeting skills
- problem solving and decision making
- quality improvement techniques
- cross-training in other roles
- self-development skills

Managers and team leaders need to develop additional skills:

- coaching and facilitation
- empathetic listening
- influencing skills
- identification of training needs
- budget preparation and management

EVALUATION

The outcomes of training and development should always be evaluated against the original objectives. Without measurement, training is too much of an act of faith, subject to doubts about effectiveness or budget cuts. So rigour at the start will pay off later. Customer perceptions of changed behaviours as well as the views of the participants, their peers and their managers can be canvassed to evaluate training effectiveness. The growth of 360 degree feedback and upward appraisal of managers has given more focus to real behaviour change, what really happens back at work. This method has worked for many of the organizations we have studied. Using this feedback approach, areas of improvement can be more accurately identified and further areas for development implemented. This should be done with the full involvement of the employee.

Finally, in evaluating the effectiveness of training and development techniques, recognize that *training produces a motivational lift*. Its energising effect can be long-lasting if people are trained and developed on a regular basis and new skills are put into practice.

An example of empowering training

Stena Line used the opportunity of a major refurbishment of one of its cross Channel ferries to harness the energy and creativity of employees in introducing a new fast food service. Following an intensely experiential training workshop of change for managers, all passenger services staff went through a three-day training programme. The aim was to draw out staff's views and put these into action. Two designers were on hand to listen to views on new uniforms and staff put forward suggestions on how they should behave to create just the right kind of informal, lively atmosphere. This was supported and encouraged by management. The third day was spent by staff giving presentations to senior management. The outcome was enthusiasm and commitment, further cemented by on-the-job coaching when the service started. Selected staff were then trained to deliver training to new staff to ensure that the process of change was self-sustaining.

9

COMMUNICATION AND EMPOWERMENT

Introduction

> **"Real communication is an attitude, it's an environment . . . It involves more listening than talking. It is a constant interactive process aimed at consensus."**
>
> **Jack Welch, CEO of G.E.**

Good communication builds knowledge and commitment; people who are involved and kept in the picture feel part of things and are able to do their jobs to the best of their ability. The opposite – secrets, being kept in the dark, receiving little regular communication – makes people feel left out, vulnerable and exposed, which fuels an 'us and them' atmosphere of mistrust.

Effective communication is both a sign of successful empowerment, and the means to ensure it happens. Regular and unrestricted communication won't happen without effort and persistence. The bigger the organization, the more thorough and systematic must be the communication. The communication process can be usefully mapped out to ensure you engage employees with differing needs at all levels and function.

GOOD COMMUNICATION MEANS GOOD LISTENING

Communication in an empowered organization will be open, two-way and frequent. There needs to be demonstrably good listening, feedback mechanisms and regular information and discussion about how the organization is doing. This sends strong messages about the value of employees. Good communication demonstrates respect for people and shows them their views and opinions are valued. This in turn leads to employees more willing to make their own decisions and to suggest ideas. Nissan UK reckon that ninety per cent of changes to its current production comes from people doing the job.

One large management development consultancy has created a programme called 'Team Listening'. The company recognizes that staff are provided with information through in-house business journals and notice boards, yet they often do not have a forum in which to discuss issues. 'Team Listening' encourages the manager to spend time in sessions with staff, during which he or she spends only five minutes talking, the rest listening.

But many organizations who have undertaken employee surveys have found that managers are not seen to listen genuinely. One company which was publicly aspiring to empowerment collected these responses from its attitude survey:

'People are sometimes taken for granted.'
'Managers do not listen to employees – especially on day-to-day gripes.'
'There are too many managers who do not understand people issues.'

If these comments are representative, managers can't be surprised that they fail to get sufficient interest in improving the quality of the organization through empowerment. Peter Wickens, former Personnel Director at Nissan UK, believes empathetic listening is the key to leadership and empowerment. Nissan puts this into practice such that it has become the model for many other companies.

Externally too, customers and suppliers need good two-way communication. Some organizations for example regularly send out a customer newsletter.

A reminder on personal communication skills
To ensure that people feel respected and understood – the basis for empowerment, demonstrate active listening:

- don't talk too much (many people do!)
- try not to interrupt
- don't complete people's sentences or anticipate what they are saying
- ask questions where you are unclear
- summarize to check your understanding
- it's better to talk face-to-face than communicate in writing, particularly on sensitive issues capable of misunderstanding

HOW POOR COMMUNICATION UNDERMINES EMPOWERMENT – AND WHAT MANAGERS SHOULD DO ABOUT IT!

- Everyone gets too busy.
  Action: Set the example by *making* time without exception. Managers' example is critical.
- Managers spend too much time at their desks and stop walking around.
  Action: Start walking!
- Information managers receive from employees isn't acted upon, so employees lose heart and stop giving information or expressing their feelings.
  Action: Regularly make a point of demonstrating ideas have been actioned.
- New ideas are stifled. People think they know better – the "Yes, but" syndrome.
  Action: Hold free thinking team sessions – no suggestions barred.
- Mechanisms to gain and distribute information are poor.

> **Action: Review the effectiveness of your communication channels.**

- Managers send out mixed messages, the words say one thing, deeds another. Commercial confidentiality is used as a means to continue to suggest a secretive 'need to know' culture.

  Action: Put a plan into effect to widen the scope of the information you talk about at team meetings.

- The 'we've had a push on communications' school of thinking. But communication must be a regular, continuous process, not a one off.

  Action: Review ways you are putting your message over. Have they become jaded?

- Information is badly presented. In these days of the information explosion there is often far too much data generated, but much of it gets ignored. Why? Because it is the wrong type of information or targeted at the wrong audience and perhaps contains jargon, or is not grouped together to make it intelligible to the reader.

  Action: Conduct a readability survey – how much is read and understood.

- Externally, people start to assume that they know their customer or supplier but do they? As needs change they may get out-of-date.

  Action: Everyone in your team is assigned a list of customers and suppliers to talk to. Draw up a checklist of items where you need to improve.

Effective communication – the catalyst for empowerment

The process of encouraging empowerment needs *open, good communication*. A major change programme within Kent County Council has allowed the organization to be successful in building communications. The catalyst for change was the 'Making Connections' communications programme which was run for 1200 senior and middle managers who were encouraged through an action learning approach to share work-related problems. This cross-functional strategy has led to a shared way of finding solutions to problems. It has resulted in greater networking and two-way communication between work groups which has contributed greatly to the empowerment process throughout the whole organization.

Ways to ensure good communication in and outside your team

It is all too easy to become insular. Front-line staff in particular can be the 'eyes and ears' for the organization.

Help your team listen to your customers – all those people in the organization and outside it whom your teams serve. Develop mechanisms to pick up what the customer is really saying – *not* what you *assume* they may want or need:

- Surveys and focus groups (at least once a year)
- Complaints
- Customer visits
- User groups and conferences

Post Office Counters uses local customer questionnaires for each outlet to set improvement goals which are relevant to each unit.

Nationwide Building Society developed an effective way of allowing senior managers to listen to the concerns of its employees. On a regular basis large groups of staff come together with a panel of two to four senior managers. The session, called 'Talkback', encourages employees to talk and debate with their managers on current issues and future plans. There is no agenda and everyone is encouraged to speak out and freely air their views.

THE ROLE OF MANAGERS IN DEVELOPING COMMUNICATIONS

Managers need to communicate information, but they also must demonstrate genuine empathy and listening. There are some systematic ways to help achieve this:

- **Carry out team briefings.** Expect and encourage questions and comment.

- **Don't leave people out whose jobs are remote – either geographically or who work different hours**. At Leeds-based Haleys Hotel and Restaurant the manager makes a point of spending time with all members of staff, irrespective of their shift patterns.

- **Regularly share information about the business as part of your day-to-day conversations.** This way you help people to understand wider business issues like costs – for example a waiter should know how much it costs to launder a napkin. This enables everyone to feel part of the business and to contribute with a wider level of knowledge.

- **Everyone has an important part to play whether it is peeling potatoes or the head waiter.** Different people have differing needs according to their experience and job. Make certain you communicate what they need and don't make assumptions about them.

- **Hold team celebrations to share successes and recognize contributors.** The Chief Executive of Lifeskills International, a personal development company, regularly holds social events such as fell walking or a summer barbecue to cement team *togetherness*.

- **Hold periodic improvement events to stimulate new ideas.** Birmingham Midshires Building

Society does this, bringing in outside speakers to promote fresh thinking.

- **Devise suggestion schemes to stimulate interest in new ideas**. Haley's Hotel and Restaurant runs a 'Captain Quality' scheme, where a staff member and a partner are invited to be a guest for the evening with an overnight stay. The employee later briefs the team on his or her impressions. Ideas are captured on a whiteboard in the staff room and act as reminders for the next month.

- **Recognize the power of personal example.** Managers need to demonstrate they are prepared to take personal responsibility for good communications.

- **Make use of all available technology**. This includes newsletters, e-mail, video conferencing, video and audio tapes. The Automobile Association, for example, sends regular audio tapes to its patrol staff to keep them up-dated. Recognize, however, that there is no substitute for face-to-face communication.

- **Communicate positive expectations.** Expect the best, reward success. Notice what is going well and give generous and specific praise and recognition.

- **Keep your lines of communication short to avoid distortion and slowing things down.** Empowered organizations avoid long chains of command.

- **Software company SCO published these maxims to all its managers:**

  1. Accept you have a prime responsibility for communication.

2. Know your objectives, understand and respect other people's.
3. Put your messages across simply and straightfor-wardly.
4. Openness and honesty breed openness and honesty in others.

- **Review your communications**. How effectively are they working? Assess: What do you communicate? How do you communicate? Where? And when? Avoid relying on one favourite means of communication.

- **Re-evaluate your personal style of communicating.** Ask for honest feedback on how you come across and how you could improve. Are you doing enough two-way communication.

- **Remember the power of body language in face-to-face dealings; some research suggests this is the major means by which we communicate.** The implications of this are the need to pay attention to: facial expression, amount of eye contact, tone of voice, and how you sit, stand.

People soon pick up how energetic or enthusiastic you are and this can be infectious. If you ignore people or keep yourself apart most of the time you will find it harder to be taken seriously in formal communications.

Team briefings
Team briefings are a systematic way of ensuring every employee receives important information about the organization. They are 'cascaded' by working groups or teams within a defined time-scale. To ensure briefings are well-run, consider the following prompts:

- Brief in person – don't be tempted to send round a piece of paper instead.

- Make it regular – at least once a month. It is better to hold very short regular sessions than protracted ones with lengthly intervals between them.

- Be factual, especially in relation to key relevant facts. Include local information, don't just put over general organizational facts. Emphasize relevant points.

- Allow time to invite questions.

- Good preparation is likely to help a good presentation.

- If you are being briefed yourself make notes and be prepared to clarify areas your team may ask you about. At Federal Express, monthly team briefings are a regular channel of communication. They are founded on the principles of feedback and employee involvement in workplace improvement.

COMMUNICATION BETWEEN TEAMS

Empowered organizations will only work well across the board if communication is strong between different groups. A valuable task for action which managers can carry out is to network with other departments and outside the organization, with customers and suppliers. A manager is a very useful communications resource to ensure expectations are clarified and that they are capable of fulfilment. Managers can be important in facilitating their teams to communicate clearly and fully with one another.

- Consider holding inter-team events to clarify expectations, build trust and avoid misunderstandings.

- Short questionnaires or surveys are a useful means to understand if needs and priorities are being met.

- Encourage differences and conflicting opinions to surface, but handle them in a way which does not become personal or accusing.

In the US, mining and construction equipment manufacturer Caterpillar experienced friction amongst teams in the early stages of empowerment. Teams were becoming frustrated because other groups were reversing decisions which they felt inappropriate. The problem was solved by each team clarifying what decisions they would make and those where they needed to refer to others. This was sytematically communicated between teams.

In OCS Smarts Group, a laundry and workwear service business, problems relating to cross-functional processes or aspects affecting several functions are addressed by network teams of volunteers from all levels of the business. Examples of the benefits the company has seen from this approach include greater awareness of how the business is run and cross-training of staff to increase skills.

Meetings

Meetings are the key means by which empowered groups keep abreast of what is going on in the organization and influence its progress. All too often, however, attendees feel frustrated by meetings – particularly those which are unstructured or too long, unclear in purpose and vague in terms of responsibilities for actions.

One reason dissatisfaction is so high is that few people take the time regularly to review the effectiveness of their meetings and decide what action needs to take place to remedy deficiencies. Empowered teams need to take time out as part of their meetings to review:

Purpose	– was everyone clear on what the meeting was about?
Relevance	– did it necessitate the involvement of all the team?
Time	– was time spent wisely?
Co-ordination	– was there effective co-ordination of the agenda and the meeting?
Contribution	– did everyone have a chance to speak? Were they listened to?
Openness and honesty	– were there any hidden agendas? How much did people speak their minds?
Actions	– were actions clear and was there real commitment to them?

To help ensure meetings are well-managed issue an agenda beforehand:

- State the time the meeting will start and end – and stick to it.
- Circulate minutes or action points quickly after the meeting, specifying who is responsible for what and by when.
- Ensure that you are a good example to others.

A case study of improving communications as part of an empowerment initiative

At the start of a big empowerment change effort, the 10,000 strong engineering division of a multi-national company set out to improve its communications considerably.

Senior managers received one-to-one coaching so that they would consciously model the more open behaviour required in the new organization. For example, managers would no longer work in a separate 'Mahogany Row' but be located in open-plan offices with their teams.

Specially appointed and trained departmental communication representatives spread the word on strategy and company issues and fed back difficulties or blocks to senior management.

Each department was asked to review the effectiveness of its communications and draw up an action plan. It was felt that communication would not improve unless managers in particular were more skilled in the principles and practices of communication. Skill development in these areas was introduced as part of a leadership programme. These skills were then developed in other groups, emphasising the message that *communication was everyone's responsibility*, not just managers or the Human Resource department. Initial results demonstrated improvement, yet it was recognized that even more effort and resources would need to be deployed as the change process gathered momentum.

10

EMPOWERMENT IN ACTION

So far we have described the elements of empowerment. We will now draw these together in examining how two organizations have worked to achieve empowerment.

Novotel

The Novotel group operates 300 hotels across 46 countries. Part of the French-based Accor group, Novotel was founded on the principle of offering the same standard of room to all customers on a global basis.

The concept was well-received by customers and the chain grew rapidly. To bring some control to a rapid programme of expansion, rigid guidelines were developed for the brand. These provided a structured framework or set of rules to which each hotel adhered strictly. Over time, what began as a flexible and customer-focused organization turned into a rigid hierarchy of administration both within each hotel and across the management structure itself.

Although the organization saw a rapid period of expansion, by 1993 senior managers recognized the opportunity and pressure to increase sales and to respond more flexibly to changing customer needs.

The first step was to revitalize the image of the brand itself which no longer appealed as strongly as it had in the past to customer tastes.

A programme of *delayering* took place which pushed down drastically the organization's levels of authority both within individual hotels and at group management level.

A critical part of regaining a customer focus has been the empowerment of the general managers of each hotel. He or she is now responsible for the running of the hotel in the manner best suited to the customer base. This is still within clear guidelines, but these are less detailed.

In order to provide support to general managers in their new roles, new training programmes have been designed called 'The School of Life'. These programmes give managers responsibility for their own development, as well as equipping them with the skills needed to coach and train their staff.

The empowerment programme is called 'Back to the Future!' An important element of this has been to encourage staff development in an organization where the traditional career path has been flattened. A four-year development plan, called 'Progress' encourages staff to work towards four levels of competencies which, it is believed, will equip them with the skills to take on increased responsibility in the workplace.

Over a twelve month period Novotel has been encouraged by the success of the programme and in a highly competitive market has seen increases in occupancy, customer satisfaction and profitability.

Glaxo Wellcome
The early 90s saw a massive period of transition for the pharmaceutical market in the UK through changes in the health service brought about by government legislation, the growing demands of customers and increased competition.

Glaxo Wellcome, the largest pharmaceutical company in the world, is the result of a recent merger of two large pharmaceutical manufacturers. Glaxo Wellcome's response to increasing changes in its environment has been to reorganize its business processes to focus on the customer. Prior to its merger with Wellcome, Glaxo began a process of re-engineering to create a greater customer awareness.

One of the outcomes of the change programme was the creation of a unified customer services department, a new initiative for the company. The department provides specialist advice and support to customers – pharmacists and medical personnel such as doctors and practice nurses. Other stakeholders include sales representatives who provide face-to-face contact with customers.

The Customer Service Department is made up of two teams each with a team leader. Both teams are supported by a team coach, a new position whose role is to provide encouragement and support the development of both individuals and the team. A manager heads the department.

As the department was started from scratch, in the first six months of its existence efforts were concentrated on recruitment and getting new systems up and running. Looking back, the departmental manager recognizes this as a difficult period of change. The turning-point came when the department created a vision and undertook an analysis of its business processes to help clarify roles and responsibilities within the team as well as defining the type of person required for each role. A set of goals was then generated by each team for itself and for the whole department.

A programme was created to help empower team members to deliver excellent customer service. Entitled 'Exceeding Customer Expectations', the programme included benchmarking visits to other organizations to establish best practice as well as skills training. An important element of the programme was the emphasis on individuals in the teams generating ideas for improvements in customer service and working practices, and their taking responsibility for driving these through to implementation.

The teams have established methods for generating feedback from their customers via annual telephone surveys, as well as a system of following up a percentage of all customer calls to gauge customer satisfaction. A 'Sounding Board' has also been set up where members of the teams and sales representatives meet on a monthly basis to bounce new ideas around and share information. The cross-fertilization of ideas and focus on the customer is also encouraged by secondments of sales representatives to work in the department for short periods.

Opportunities for learning and self-development have been expanded. Every individual has a personal development plan and spends time with the team coach for help in achieving their plan.

Recent customer surveys have indicated a growing level of satisfaction amongst customers with the service the department provides. Feedback from members of the department indicates that although at times the establishment of the department has been difficult, particularly as the organization was undergoing a period of change at the same time, there is a growing feeling of empowerment and focus on the customer as a result of the process.

11

THE LIBERATING FORCES OF CHANGE

The examples given in the last chapter and throughout this book serve to suggest the complexity of making empowerment happen in organizations today. Many organizations have a history and culture which impede empowerment.

Most managers can buy into the concept, but many fail actually to give it sufficient active support during implementation. When things start to happen to them they tend to retreat to known methods of tight control – *exactly the reverse of what is needed*. They may also start to feel anxious that they are no longer 'doing their job properly' or even worse, that their jobs are no longer really there.

Equally, many employees are at first wary of the additional responsibility or workload. They worry about making mistakes or about whether they have sufficient knowledge and overview of the situation to make decisions which they have never made before.

The growing number of organizations that do bring these forces together experience a powerful and liberating effect. **Empowerment can only come about when all three components – the organization, the manager and the individual are working in a complementary and supportive manner to increase the velocity of change:**

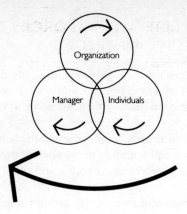

If the three work together, empowerment becomes the accelerator of change, but if one or more moves slowly or in a different direction, the wheels grind to a halt, or move only fractionally. This checklist of indications of empowerment will enable you to draw up action points to keep empowerment moving forward.

The Organization
Foster an empowered environment through:

- Making clear the direction and values of the organization and encouraging employees to own these by contributing to, setting and maintaining them.
- Valuing open and honest two-way communication – and practising it regularly.
- Encouraging learning and discouraging blame.
- Rewarding effort and achievement fairly, allowing employees to contribute.
- Allowing employees to learn from their mistakes and encouraging people to speak out.
- Promoting the value of working together and sharing responsibility.
- Creating a customer focus.

Managers

Empowered managers:

- Make explicit through their behaviour their active support of empowerment and confidence in their colleagues' abilities – they listen, trust and respect others.
- Share information, knowledge and responsibility.
- Facilitate others in their personal development.
- Encourage others to share ideas and take appropriate risks.
- Provide freedom and clarify agreed boundaries with their team members.

Individuals

Empowered individuals:

- Recognize that they have a choice and are accountable for what they do.
- Seek to understand the big picture and how they fit into it.
- Welcome the opportunity to learn and take on new rolés.
- Are prepared to experiment.
- Are ready to challenge what they feel is wrong.
- Take responsibility for their career and personal achievement.
- Recognize success in other people and are prepared to support them.

When all three forces meet, it is possible to harness everyone's energy to beneficial effect on the organization and the individual.

Jack Welch at GE sums up empowerment in the new GE he has initiated: *'People really do take ideas from A to B. In the old culture if you had an idea you'd keep it.'* It is this empowered sharing and freeing up the potential of its people which allows GE's performance to keep on improving despite rapid change.

Numerous examples world-wide demonstrate that the path to empowerment is steep, and unless you are prepared for this journey, empowerment will indeed become just another fad. We hope this book will have helped you make a more informed choice on whether empowerment is right for your organization. Substantial productivity and profitability gains, greater customer satisfaction and employee involvement are prizes worth attaining.

PERFECT CUSTOMER CARE

Ted Johns

The only customers truly worth having are regular customers – those who come back to buy again and again. But they won't come back with those valuable repeat orders unless you know how to look after them, how to provide what they want plus a bit extra, and how to add value to every transaction. Everyone in the firm, from the boss to the shopfloor worker, has a part to play in converting a one-time customer, whether internal or external, into a thoroughly satisfied client whose renewed orders will provide the basis of your success.

Perfect Customer Care provides companies big and small with the answers to some of the most important business questions of the 1990s.

£5.99

ISBN 0–7126–5912–9

PERFECT TIME MANAGEMENT

Ted Johns

Managing your time effectively means adding value to everything you do. This book will help you to master the techniques and skills essential to grasping control of your time and your life.

If you can cut down the time you spend meeting people, talking on the 'phone, writing and reading reports and answering subordinates' questions, you can use the time saved for creative work and the really important elements of your job. Learn how to deal with interruptions, manage the boss and cut down on meetings time – above all, how to minimize paperwork. You'll be amazed how following a few simple guidelines will improve the quality of both your working life and your leisure time.

£5.99

ISBN 0–7126–5549–2

THE PERFECT NEGOTIATION

Gavin Kennedy

The ability to negotiate effectively is a vital skill required in business and everyday situations.

Whether you are negotiating over a business deal, a pay rise, a difference of opinion between manager and staff, or the price of a new house or car, this invaluable book, written by one of Europe's leading experts in negotiation, will help you to get a better deal every time, and avoid costly mistakes.

£5.99

ISBN 0–7126–5465–8

PERFECT PR

Marie Jennings

We are all communicators – all the time. It is vitally important to consider what we are communicating, and whether or not we are being effective. Public relations is increasingly recognized as an important business tool, but it is a personal tool as well. Understanding PR and how to make it work for you as well as for your company will help you get what you want from your life.

Perfect PR helps you to examine yourself as a communicator. It gives a bird's-eye view of PR, describes the various techniques involved, and shows you how to make the most of them.

Covering PR for individuals, companies, products and charities, this is the perfect book for anyone who has a job of promotion to do, whatever the subject.

£5.99

ISBN 0–09–950811–7

PERFECT MARKETING

Louella Miles

Every company wants sustainable growth and over the years it has been marketing that has helped them to achieve it. Yet marketing suffers a muddled identity, often confused with selling and advertising.

This book sets the record straight. It looks at marketing as a whole and at each of its constituent parts, offering guidance on what can be achieved realistically and how to measure results. It examines the industry of the 90s, the impact of new technology, the role of innovation and how marketers can plan not just for survival but for growth.

£5.99

ISBN 0–09–950521–5

THE PERFECT BUSINESS PLAN

Ron Johnson

A really professional business plan is crucial to success. This book provides a planning framework and shows you how to complete it for your own business in 100 easy to follow stages.

Business planning will help you to make better decisions today, taking into account as many of the relevant factors as possible. A carefully prepared business plan is essential to the people who will put money into the business, to those who will lend it money, and above all to the people who carry out its day to day management.

£5.99

ISBN 0–7126–5524–7

PERFECT PERSONAL FINANCE

Marie Jennings

We all need to use money - every day of our lives. It is important to understand the simple principles which can help us to use money effectively, so that it can play its rightful part in enabling us to lead the sort of life we want.

This book helps you to examine yourself and your money. It shows how to identify what you want from your life and how to use all your resources – time, energy and money – to achieve your personal potential. Written in a clear, jargon-free style, *Perfect Personal Finance* goes to the heart of money management and signposts ways to get further advice if you want to go into the subject more deeply.

£5.99

ISBN 0–09–963851–7